VIBRATING ABUNDANCE

Creating Wealth from the Inside

Kidest OM

Vibrating Abundance: Creating Wealth from the Inside by Kidest OM

3rd Edition

All rights reserved. Copyright © by Kidest OM 2009.

No part of this book shall be reproduced, stored in a retrieval system, or transmitted by any means – electronic, mechanical, photocopying, recording, or otherwise – without written permission from the author.

ISBN: 1495493334
ISBN-13: 978-1495493331

SELF RESPONSIBLITY

The author of this material does not dispense medical advice or prescribe the use of any technique as a form of professional therapeutic treatment for physical, emotional, psychological, or medical conditions without the advice of an appropriate qualified health practitioner or physician, either directly or indirectly. The intent of the author is only to offer information of a general nature. In the event you use any of the information in this material for yourself, which is your right, the author assumes no responsibility for your choices or actions. By using the material, you assume and accept full responsibility for any and all outcomes you experience.

You cannot create lasting change without expanding out of the consciousness that brought forth the things you want changed.

- Kidest OM

CONTENTS

INTRODUCTION	9
VIBRATING ABUNDANCE	12
PART I – PREMISE OF WORKBOOK	15
ABUNDANCE	17
MONEY	20
EXPOSING YOUR RULE-SETS	21
THE PROCESS	23
THE NATURE OF SIMULTANEOUS FREQUENCY DOMAINS	28
PART II – THE WORKBOOK	31
DAILY EXERCISES	33
PART III: YOUR NEW PATTERN	161
DECLARATION OF INNER POWER	165
NEW MONEY THOUGHTS	167
ABUNDANT THOUGHTS	168
MORE POSITIVE MONEY BELIEFS	171
ANTICIPATING ABUNDANCE	181

INTRODUCTION

The goal of this workbook is to provide you with a focused avenue and space for shifting your relationship to prosperity and abundance. While everyone will benefit from committing to a dedicated focus on shifting experiences of abundance and prosperity to a more positive flow, what will maximize your benefit, is having already familiarized yourself with principles of intentional or deliberate reality creation.

This workbook assumes that you already have a level of understanding on these concepts and only briefly summarizes some components of reality creation.

To get the most out of the focus this workbook provides, you must let go of having some external outcome in mind. Let your focus during the course of this workbook be to shift and stabilize yourself into a new perspective and energy when it comes to abundance, money, and prosperity. Since it is the interior of your being that is the source of your external reality, let yourself commit to just focusing on the interior – to just reorganizing the internal space of your thoughts, beliefs, emotions and so on.

By solely intending to focus all of your energy in creating a shift in consciousness, you'll create a concentrated coherent intention that will become the basis of experiencing a powerful shift throughout your entire being. It is this all-inclusive interior change that will allow you to easily, effortlessly and consistently experience a new flow of abundance.

When attention is split into internal and external focus or when it is solely focused on the external, where you find yourself somewhat paying attention to your thoughts and somewhat paying attention to manifestation or not at all paying attention to your internal world, your signal to the Universal Field is incoherent, wobbly, and inconsistent. So your results are wobbly, confusing, unpredictable and inconsistent.

The predictability in your successful manifestation of your desired abundance comes from a stable shift, change and reorganization of your interior, your internal environment of thoughts, beliefs, emotions and so on. So for the duration of this workbook and anytime you bring yourself back to playing and working at shifting consciousness in some desired area, your goal must be to do just that.

To say "I'm going to shift my consciousness in this area for the sake of just shifting my consciousness in this area" brings a different intensity of focus on your interior than to say "I'm going to shift my consciousness in this area so that I can quadruple my income" – the latter will have you splitting your focus so that you can't help but find yourself checking again and again for external evidence on your progress.

You want to bring that sole intense focus into your work on changing yourself, changing your consciousness because that is what will allow you to accomplish the transformation in an uninterrupted and undistracted way.

Just as the caterpillar must cocoon itself to transform into a butterfly, you must cocoon yourself from anything related to the outside world as it relates to your outcome and solely focus on transforming your interior, your psychological, emotional and energetic world. In doing that, you will emerge from your work as a new being and so find yourself experiencing an entirely new world as it relates to abundance, prosperity and money in general.

VIBRATING ABUNDANCE

Reality is created from the inside. Everything you experience is an outcome of the energy that you are being, and the energy that you are being is formed by the patterns of thinking and feeling you have habituated as your norm. The focus of this workbook is to take you through a set of paradigm shifting information and exercises so that you can expand your flow of abundance from the inside out. The work book offers you new ways of looking at your power to attract and allow abundance in all forms.

Each day you are provided with thoughts that allow you to look at your financial flow from a new perspective. The thoughts presented are resonating at a specific frequency. Your goal is to begin to get yourself consistently living from the frequency of the streams of thinking and feeling presented in this workbook and to expand your energetic set-point.

As you entertain these new ideas and practice the exercises offered over the course of 40 days, you will set into motion the shift in consciousness necessary to bring about any lasting change in your physical experience. As your consciousness changes, as your rehearsed patterns of thinking and feeling shift into new habituated patterns of thinking and feeling, and you stabilize in a new energetic resonance, your flow of abundance will noticeably shift.

You CAN allow your flow of prosperity to expand from the inside out. You CAN create an outrageous stream of wealth in all areas of your life.

PART I – PREMISE OF WORKBOOK

Your abundance is a creation of your Consciousness.

Your materialized abundance is an indicator of your dominant patterns of emotionalized thought.

Your materialized abundance is a result of the beliefs you have practiced about money, prosperity, and wealth.

Your manifested prosperity is your practiced patterns of thought around money crystallized.

Your manifested abundance is the essence of your thoughts solidified.

Your abundance is an outcome or out-picturing of your thoughts.

Your abundance can expand in proportion to your practiced patterns of thoughts.

You CAN change your materialized abundance naturally by changing your vibration, by making a shift in consciousness.

• • •

The premises outlined highlight the necessity of taking full ownership of what you experience as your current flow of abundance. There cannot be an inkling of powerlessness in your relationship to abundance. It is when you take full responsibility and ownership for your current experience that you give yourself the power and energy to move yourself into a new realm of consciousness, into a new realm of thought and feeling.

By integrating the essence of what's outlined in the premise and integrating within yourself perspectives that resonate in the realm of creative ownership, you have taken the first step in bringing about a deliberate and intentional shift in the reality you are living.

ABUNDANCE

All that you experience in and as your physical reality is a creation of your Consciousness. As you look out through your physical apparatus into this manifested world, all that confronts you are only the ideas you hold about who you are and what this physical time-space environment is. Throughout your physically focused experience you have accumulated thoughts, learned beliefs, and have stabilized in a range of emotions about the nature of abundance, the nature of your being, and the source of all that you experience. And it is these line up of well-rehearsed beliefs, feelings and ideas that mold the experiences you live out in and as your personal reality.

The reality field in your view is subject to instantaneous change. All of that which appears on your screen of experience can change for the better as you adjust the ideas you have encoded onto your consciousness-matrix. And it is this inner change, this shift in consciousness, that you want to mobilize by exposing yourself to and tuning into ideas that are vibrating at the frequency of the experiences you desire to make manifest.

Every idea in existence is a pattern of energy vibrating at a specific frequency, and like ideas, ideas of similar or the same vibrational density, have the tendency to create unique fields of experience. The frequency domain you access and draw your physical reality out of is a domain of like ideas, of like patterns of energy vibrating as specific frequencies. The frequency domain or reality field of abundance is quite different from the frequency domain or vibrational density of lack and scarcity. These are domains made up of distinctly different thoughts, emotions, expectations, assumptions, stories, themes, epochs, meme's and so on. What's more is, the vibration of your own being is unique to the reality domain that you tune into and create out of. The abundant you is vibrating at quite a different frequency than the you that experiences lack and scarcity.

Nothing about your physical experience is solid and unchanging. Nothing about your personal reality is static and confined to remain as it right now appears. You are not limited to what appears to be real to you right now. As you adjust the vibration of the ideas you hold, your expectations and definitions of what physical reality is and all that it can become, as well as your definitions of who and what you are, how and in what ways the experiences on your screen change will astound you.

You are not limited by circumstances and conditions outside of you. You are not confined and bound by experiences and events external to you. All that limits your experiences of physical reality, all that determines which frequency-stream you tune into and make manifest as your personal world and life story, are the ideas, web of beliefs, and expectations you have formed based on the information you have passively and by default integrated into the vibrational lens through which you experience this time-space environment.

What you experience as abundance is the innate nature of this time-space environment. Abundance is the premise of That which you experience as your Universe. There is only abundance in its myriad of forms or your resistance to it in the thoughts and ideas you have rehearsed thus far into your physical focus. That needs repeating – you are either experiencing your innate abundance or you are experiencing your resistance to your innate abundance.

Abundance is not what you have, it is who you are. Abundance is your true nature, the natural state of the Consciousness that is the real You. And as you tune into "higher" ideas, as you attune yourself to ideas of a different vibrational density, all the abundance that you truly are will become in and as your visible world.

Know this and own this with every fiber of your being. Allow yourself to fully integrate the recognition that your true nature, your core essence, the fabric of your being is endless abundance.

You are the sole author of all that you make manifest in and as your time-space environment.

MONEY

Abundance is myriad in its forms. Yet for most who are physically focused, the subject of great resistance is not the lack of trees, oxygen or ocean in this time-space environment but rather the flow of money into and out of their personal experience. So it is money and financial prosperity, and the perceived lack of it that is addressed in the following pages of this workbook.

However, you can easily replace the subject of money and financial prosperity for an area of focus that you are more interested in. The premises and ideas in this workbook are easily transferable and apply to any aspect of your personal reality where you want to experience a shift in consciousness.

EXPOSING YOUR RULE-SETS

What exactly is money? What is money made of? What is your criteria for having dollars? What do you believe it takes to have money and keep it coming? How many days, months does it take? How much work does it take? How easy or hard will it be? How rapidly can you materialize money? How long do you believe it takes to increase your cash flow? What is the source of your financial prosperity? Who is the source of your financial prosperity?

Ask yourself these questions and more questions like them. Get a deeper look at the rule-sets you've created for yourself – the thought parameters you've practiced about financial prosperity and what it takes to express abundance. This is a crucial step in your achieving a lasting shift in consciousness. You must expose your current psychological and emotional map around money, finances, investments, income, cash flow, savings, payments, sales, pricing and all else associated with prosperity.

How you have psychologically and emotionally mapped yourself to money and everything associated with it is what is determining your vibration as it relates to it. Your current internal representations, the images and associations you've formed throughout your life around money and all things related to money is what's getting you the results you are getting. You will always create and materialize your experiences within the boundaries of your beliefs so it's critical that you expose and make visible these beliefs to yourself.

These rule-sets are not facts. They are not solid unchangeable realities. They are only thoughts that have been practiced and believed-in in your lifetime. They are only thoughts that you have inherited and integrated into your blueprint for this reality. They are only thoughts, instructions that have been used to translate energy into form. They are only as valid and powerful as you make them. As you expose these patterns, as you bring them into your conscious awareness for evaluation and illumination, you'll shed the density that has been keeping you from experiencing your true nature, your true core vibration which is that of appreciative abundance – endless and ever-expanding abundance.

Your materialized abundance will always come in response to your practiced patterns of thought – to the invisible expectations you've formed based on information you've gathered in your physical experience. The more you make these beliefs or manufactured expectations visible to yourself, the more you can deliberately change them so that getting the results you want is natural and effortless.

> *"Sitting silently, doing nothing,*
> *The spring comes*
> *And the grass grows by itself"* - Osho

THE PROCESS

Everything you think manifests itself as the circumstances and conditions of your physical life. Your materialized abundance is no exception to this universal creative process.

This workbook is designed to help you access and form new patterns of thought and so new feelings around your sense of wealth, so you can begin to experience your natural and unfailing abundance.

Your dominant thoughts, your dominant vibrational out-put, have everything to do with why your prosperity appears as it does, for above all else, your abundance has come about in response first and foremost to the thoughts you think. It's imperative that you accept the premise "my thoughts and feelings create my abundance".

In this lifetime, you have created many thought patterns and emotional responses around money, work, cost, expense, value, spending, and around many other aspects of your abundance. And these practiced thought patterns are constantly playing on loop in your mind. You have an ongoing silent story you tell about your prosperity in the privacy of your own mind.

Every time you sit to pay a bill, you are thinking thoughts and having an emotional response. Every time you go to do your groceries, you are thinking thoughts and having emotional responses. Every time you want to buy something new, you are thinking thoughts and having the corresponding emotional response. Every time you receive a cheque or a deposit, you are thinking thoughts and generating those well-rehearsed emotions around receiving money. Every time you go to buy coffee, you are thinking thoughts. Every time you walk by a shop window, you are thinking thoughts. Everything you do, you do so in the constant and endless company of your thoughts.

If experiencing your natural abundance is your goal, if expanding your level of wealth is your goal, then it's important that your repetitive thoughts support that goal rather than contradict it. For in this attraction-based Universe, the thoughts you repeatedly think and the emotions they evoke within you have more power to bring you the results you want in a permanent and effortless way than any action based effort you involve yourself in.

Your goals do not need to feel like a

struggle. Your process of achievement on every subject need not feel like a struggle. In fact, the only reason that it does feel like a struggle is because you have contradictory thoughts playing in your mind every step of the way. You have mental resistance built up, and that kind of resistance is the only reason why your results are slow to come and difficult to maintain.

Working with your thought patterns is essentially treating the root cause of your manifested world rather than trying to adjust the materialized outcome.

This workbook contains a series of exercises for you to engage in daily over the next 40 days. As you go through the workbook you will expose your negative practiced patterns of thought to yourself, and as you practice and create new patterns of thinking, you will shift your consciousness to allow what you want to materialize.

Engage yourself in this workbook daily. Commit to change your inner template. Do all the exercises and allow yourself to dwell on and practice the new thoughts you are offered. For as you do, you will begin to think in a completely new way about abundance and will experience the immediate and long-term effects of that shift in your consciousness. You will begin to feel good about money in many ways, and feeling good is always the prime indicator of true and lasting fulfillment.

You can be assured and confident about your endless and abundant supply of money. You can resolutely declare that you are abundant and prosperous and know that to be the truth with every fiber of your being. You can love money. You can appreciate money. You can embrace abundant flow. You can enjoy money with unadulterated joy. You can bask in the glow of your innate abundance every day. You can know in the core of your being that you are always and at all times flourishing in abundance and being washed by a cosmic rain of abundance. However you conceive of that abundance, you know that you know that you know that you have limitless access to it.

You may wonder why 40 days. It takes repeated exposure to an idea to solidify and integrate that new idea into your consciousness. You want these ideas, these thoughts to take shape in your own consciousness. It is through repeated contact with new ideas that they become familiar and second-nature to you. When you consistently give a new idea your attention, you flow energy into that idea until it is dense enough for it to be integrated into your conscious outlook.

Repetition is and has been the pattern of everything you've learned. Everything you right now know is an idea you've repeatedly entertained and accepted. So the integration process requires your unbroken attention for a given period of time where you again and again expose yourself to new ideas and mentally and emotionally rehearse those new ideas until they become your own.

Both in the traditions of the East and the West, 40 days is held to be the length of time necessary to set such a transformation of consciousness into motion. And so that rule-set is being applied to this workbook also. It's important that you go through this workbook with perfect continuity at least the first time through. After your first time through the material you can measure for yourself the level of change you feel internally and reassess whether or not to continue on with the committed focus to transform yourself.

THE NATURE OF SIMULTANEOUS FREQUENCY DOMAINS

That you exist in a Unified Field of Infinite Possibility is an ever-emerging stream of understanding making itself known in your current time-space environment. In your powerful and ever-present Now exist all possibilities, all outcomes, and all possible versions of your own unique pattern of self.

There is already an abundant and prosperous you in this powerful instant. There is already a reality in existence right now in which you are an expression of prosperity in all forms. And it is the signal of this unique you that you are gently tuning yourself into to create and participate in the already existing reality of abundance that you are preferring to experience.

You are a multi-dimensional consciousness experiencing the nature of physical focus. You are not a limited being having to hammer a desired reality into manifestation. Your power rests in your ability to vibrate at and attune your focus to the frequency domain, the unique vibrational density, of your preferred stream of experience. Know for yourself that this preferred stream of experience is already in existence just like your favorite television or radio program is playing on your favorite channel whether you've tuned into that channel or not. Think of reality creation as reality surfing, you are tuning away from one reality and tuning into a different reality. You are not having to create an entirely new channel, rather you are tuning into a channel that already exists right here and now. Shifting consciousness, shifting reality is less work than you think. Make the shift easy on and for yourself. This responsive time-space environment that you experience as your physical Universe is ever sensitive and immediate to the shifts in frequency you generate within yourself.

You are the sole author, definer, and perceiver of all that you make manifest in and as your personal physical reality.

PART II – THE WORKBOOK

Each day contains a thought for you to contemplate followed by exercises for you to take part in as you go on about your day. There is a morning process and an evening process you take yourself through over the course of 40 days. If the ideas offered in this workbook are new for you, you can take yourself through the workbook multiple times and repeat the process until you feel the shift in consciousness within yourself. You'll know when you've changed, you'll feel the difference and you'll easily be able to tell that you are a new you, a different you.

Ideally you'll do the morning process first thing in the morning so that you begin to tune into and steer yourself toward this new way of thinking when your mind or brain waves are still in receptive mode.

For the same reason, it's ideal to do the evening process before you go to sleep. Processing information when your brain/mind is least active and preoccupied, means you'll be able to give this material the kind of distraction-free attention that's necessary to make a shift in your consciousness.

Things you'll need:

1. This workbook.
2. Your commitment to change.
3. A journal to process this information, practice the new thoughts, and keep a record of your insights.

DAILY EXERCISES

THOUGHT OF THE DAY

Each day contains a train of thought for you to contemplate and consider. The best way to shift your consciousness on a given subject is to shift your belief system around that subject – build a new understanding of what your money or abundance is and how it comes into your experience. These daily thoughts are aimed at doing just that by offering you a new way of looking and thinking about your abundance. When you transform your mind, you absolutely transform everything outside of it.

PROSPERITY SPREE

Most people want to have an abundance of dollars but wouldn't know what to do with the money beyond the obvious of buying the house and cars, and paying off "debt" once it shows up. The prosperity spree is a game to expand your mind about the kinds of things you can put your dollars toward. It expands your imagination. It expands your idea of what you can have. It gets you to think outside of your current prosperity box. It gets you to think big and then it gets you to think bigger. Each day offers you a cheque from the Universe that you spend toward whatever desired item or experience you would like to create for yourself. Have fun with this. Be bold. Be playful. Be ridiculous. Be obnoxious. Be imaginative. Use your money to get everything you want and then use it to finance building a colony on Mars or making Venus inhabitable or building stargates that let you travel into other galaxies. It's your money to do with whatever you please and there's not a limit or restriction placed on you around how you spend it. Think big and then think bigger and then think even bigger and keep going.

NEW THOUGHTS TO PRACTICE

There is a glossary of affirmation-like thoughts you can engage in at the end of this section. Let yourself cycle these thoughts. Combined with the daily thought you contemplate, the new thoughts you practice will allow you to form and radiate a new understanding. Look to these new thoughts when you're feeling contraction or having a negative emotional response of any intensity on the subject of your abundance. If other new thoughts about abundance come to you, add them to your list and keep building your database of new patterns of thinking.

PAYING ATTENTION

Throughout each day it's important to pay attention to the thoughts you are thinking around money. Where ever you are, set the intention to be aware of what you're thinking. Your emotions will always indicate to you the quality or essence of your thoughts so use your emotions to tell you what your balance of thinking is on the subject of money. If you are feeling negative emotion at any point during the day, this negative emotion is indicating to you that you are thinking thoughts in opposition to who you truly are and what you are really wanting to experience.

VISUALIZE/DAY DREAM

Visualizing is a great way to radiate the kind of energy that is in line with what you want. You cannot get to a sense of feeling abundant when your constant focus is the cash-flow you have accumulated many negative feelings around. So visualization is a great way to take yourself into the energy of your desired wealth. Build your images of abundance, wealth, prosperity. Picture what it would be like if you had it all, however you define you "having it all".

What will it feel like when you reach your goal? What kind of things will you do and have? What does your being wealthy look like? What would you hear? What would you see? What would you do day after day, month after month, year after year?

Spend five minutes or so visualizing your new sense of abundance. Feel the feelings. Picture yourself with truckloads of dollars. Picture it raining money. Picture yourself swimming in an ocean of wealth. What will people say to you when they see you? What will you say to yourself when you do some online banking? Will you have investments? Will you have assistants? What are all the components of your abundant, prosperous life as a wealthy individual?

Light Stream Visualization: Picture yourself connected with every being on the planet through a bright stream of light. This is your human network. Picture that this light stream is moving through all points of consciousness, all the billions of people on the planet. It's overflowing. It's endless. It never ceases. Recognize that right in this very instant there are billions of people that you are a channel of wealth to and that are a channel of wealth to you. Dwell on the thought that there are innumerable channels for how abundance can flow to you and through you.

Now expand out into the cosmos and picture this light stream connecting you to points of consciousness across galaxies known and unknown to you. Let yourself stay in this awareness of having a vast network spanning out into galaxies far and away and into dimensions beyond physical reality. Let yourself know how connected you are all day every day.

I-HAVE-IT LIST

Often times, through habit, you may focus on what you perceive to be "wrong" with your finances. By default the mind wonders and focuses on everything you don't like about your current financial state. Take this moment to think about everything that is right with your dollars right now just as it is. Deliberately bring yourself to focus on what you like about what you have, what you love about what you right now have. What is the money you have right now allowing you to do? What's going right for you? What's working for you? Where are you already meeting your financial needs? Where are you already successful in your ability to provide for yourself? Where are you already attracting financial fulfilment?

Deliberately train yourself into positive focus. Not only will this shift your dominant thought patterns but it will also shift the energy or essence you radiate outward which is your point of asking.

POSITIVE PROJECTION

By default your physical mind has a trained tendency to anticipate lack and scarcity. You can thank the survival programs that have ensured survival of the human species for that. The physical mind's constant guardianship on your safety and security on all levels, from physical to financial to emotional to spiritual and so on is a useful mechanism. That said, it is a system of thinking that you have to direct or soothe so that you can live from your higher mind.

When you catch yourself thinking about a future moment in which you just might not have enough money, that you might run out, practice deliberately projecting a positive future. Anticipate abundance. Train yourself into positive future expectations.

APPRECIATING

The energy of appreciation is one of the highest frequencies you can access and attune yourself to deliberately. The higher the energies you attune to, the more effortlessly and fluidly the things you are wanting flow into your experience.

Everything in your view right now has come in response to what you've been radiating or vibrating. Everything that has manifested as your dollars, as your home, as your car, as your endless list of "stuff" has come in response to your need and expectation. Every particle that is right now vibrating in your view is there because of your vibrational offering, the energy you've been radiating outward up until this point. Appreciate what's in front of you. Appreciate every particle that has shown up for your enjoyment. Appreciate the services that you are receiving in this very instant, the electricity, the water source, the beings who built your home, the beings who made your clothes and shoes. Appreciate your endless chain of abundance. Expand your mind and train yourself to anchor the energy of appreciation in your being.

SUGGESTED GUIDELINES

1)   As a rule, it's important to keep your deliberate effort to shift your consciousness on your chosen subject to yourself. Keep it as your secret so as not to introduce the negative patterns of thought active in other's into your efforts. This is your work and yours alone so mind the kind of input you allow into your efforts. Be mindful of who and in what way you share your commitment to make the internal shift with.

2)   These efforts aren't about making anything happen. You no more have to make what you're wanting happen than you have to pull the grass out of the ground or manually rotate the earth on its axis. There are natural laws at work here and you are merely working with those laws by releasing your practiced patterns of resistance. You really don't need to hammer anything into place so let your focus only be on changing your patterns of thought, shifting your vibration. The natural outcome of fulfillment is inevitable.

3) Keep conscious note that appreciation of all the things you already have on every subject is the quickest way to open your energy channels and increase the flow. Resistance in the way of critical thoughts, doubtful thoughts, thoughts about being stuck, insecure thoughts, obsessive thoughts, judgmental thoughts and the like only serve to block or pinch off the flow of universal energy. Keep appreciating the things that have already shown up in your experience no matter how much time has gone since they showed up. This will keep you open and receptive. Appreciate! Appreciate! Appreciate!

4) Keep your attention on the Cause of everything you experience. Do not be swayed by the outcomes, the conditions currently manifested around you. All conditions and circumstances are rapidly changing right in this instant, they are dissolving in the instant you decide to flow your energy elsewhere. The Cause is always your consciousness, and the thoughts you have encoded yourself with. Resolve to work at the level of Cause and let nothing distract you from the focused work. No manifestation is important enough for you to take your attention off of shifting and reorganizing your interior.

5) Relieve yourself from determining or deciding how your desires will manifest. The HOW is none of your business. Do you have to think about how you're going to make the earth spin on its axis at all hours of the day? No. Thinking about the HOW from your current vantage point is comparable of worrying all day everyday how you're going to make the earth spin on its own axis. Allow the Universe, from its broader all-seeing and infinitely intelligent vantage point, to flow it to you through easy and accessible channels. It's not your work to figure out "how" anything will come to you or materialize into your view. Your only job is to ask through the thoughts you radiate and then joyfully get out of the way.

6) Remind yourself that fulfillment is your birthright for the simple reason that you exist. There is absolutely nothing that you cannot become or materialize. "Impossible" is not a word or concept known by the energy that builds this Universe. Line yourself up to that omni-possibility. If life, if this Universe has inspired you to conceive of a desire, that desire can absolutely materialize. There are no exceptions.

7) Take time out of the equation. The only place is here and the only time is now. Whatever your desire, it can only materialize in the Now. There is no future moment. There is no future time of tomorrow, later, or "in six months" for your desire to be visible to you. The only place and time for it to materialize, is right here and right now. Be mindful of the mental tendency to futurize and set up a condition of time for materialization. Now is all there is.

8) Think of this 40 day process as a way to "upgrade" your mental operating system. It's really not anything more mystical or abstract. You're simply re-writing the thoughts you've embedded or programmed your mind with up until now.

9) Be consistent and be patient with yourself and your practice. It takes a buildup of energy in consciousness to materialize into the physical so let your intention be to make that necessary shift in consciousness. Bring yourself to a new level of thinking and feeling consistently. Allow yourself to take in information along the lines of creating change from the inside out. There are endless resources and information available that you can make use of to fill your mind with the type of thoughts necessary to make such a shift permanently.

10) Bring yourself to keep focusing on what it is that you do want. Decide to supply and apply your power, your energy only to what it is you're wanting to see. Commit to yourself and your vision. Say to yourself each day "today, no matter where I go or what I do, I choose to flow my energy only to those things I am wanting. I choose my vision." You are always radiating the energy of the thing that has your attention the most, so let what captivates you be the thing that you want.

• • •

And most importantly, enjoy your transformative journey and lovingly appreciate and acknowledge yourself for your decision, commitment and consistent practice. Your success is inevitable.

DAY 1

THOUGHT of the day: Wealth or the expression of it in your life is only an indicator of your wealth consciousness, the habit of thoughts you've formed around the subject of money, abundance, and prosperity. As you expand your ideas of what you can have, what you can be, and what you can do in this experience, and release your resistance to abundance by releasing the limited beliefs you've been holding, the expansion in your consciousness around money will naturally materialize into an increased flow of dollars and a freer relationship with money altogether. It is all in the thoughts you have practiced. It's all in the consciousness you maintain. Change your thoughts through deliberate effort and practice, and you change your reality.

PROSPERITY SPREE: Spend your daily cheque below from the Universe on new items.

VIBRATING ⊙ ABUNDANCE		
	DATE: _____	
PAY TO THE ORDER OF		$5,000
	FIVE THOUSAND	/100 DOLLARS
Universe INC. 444 Abundance Way Billionaire View, CA 000000		*The Universe* AUTHORIZED SIGNATURE
	⑈111222⑈ ⑆33⑉3444⑈ ⑆555	

Money as Acknowledgment: Remind

yourself today that there is no such thing as cost, expense, bill, or payment. Whatever you purchase today, whatever your money flows toward, your out-flow is a part of the abundance cycle. Remind yourself as you go about your day, that all there is, is a gesture of acknowledgment for the services and items you are receiving. Money is a way of saying "thank you for these services and goods" for everything you are receiving.

Your I-Have-it List: What are all the ways that you are already abundant? Take a moment today to make a list of everything you have in your life that benefits you – from the clothes you wear, the dollars and cents in your wallet or account, to the dishes in your cupboard, take a moment to take stalk of the abundance already in your experience. Give your attention to what it is you already have.

POSITIVE PROJECTION: If you notice your mind projecting a future time of lack, create and use "what if" statements like the following to anticipate abundance:

What if more money right now comes to me from various unexpected channels?
What if more money right now comes through my created channels?

What if there are more ways than I know for money to come into my life right in this instant?

What if the Universe uses the over 6.9 billion channels I'm connected to, to yield prosperity to me?

What if my accounts never even go below $_____?

What if I always have more money streaming in?

What if I remember that I am an Infinite Being with infinite resources?

APPRECIATE! APPRECIATE! APPRECIATE!

::: YOU HAVE MORE THAN ENOUGH OF EVERYTHING FOR TODAY! :::

DAY 2

THOUGHT of the day: For many people there's an undercurrent of great resistance around the topic of money. There aren't many people that go around exclaiming "I love money". This resistance has nothing to do with the colored paper and decorated coin itself, but rather the sense of lack-fullness or not enough-ness or the feeling of running out of money that many individuals grapple with.

The fear of not having enough, or feeling guilty for having more than someone else, or the feeling of frustration for not being able to hold onto money, are all constant stories that play out in many minds. All of these stories have a negative feel attached to them. And it is this negative feel that indicates to you that you are contradicting your true nature of abundance through practicing these types of thoughts. Every thought you think, is a thought you practice.

Money is a wonderful symbol. Money is a wonderful way to exchange goods and services. Money is made of the very thing that everything else is made of – it's just another form of energy, particles in constant motion.

People aren't struggling with money, they are struggling with their ideas of what money is and how much money can come into their experience. Often times, when you want something but have difficulty materializing it, you begin to form a negative view of the object, and that negative attitude keeps the very thing you want away. Money itself is neutral and impersonal. It is with your own ideas about money that you must do your work.

Your mantra for today: "I love money and money loves me."

PROSPERITY SPREE: Spend your daily cheque from the Universe on new items.

VIBRATING ⊙ ABUNDANCE	
	DATE: _____
PAY TO THE ORDER OF	$10,000
TEN THOUSAND	/100 DOLLARS
Universe INC. 444 Abundance Way Billionaire View, CA 000000	*The Universe* AUTHORIZED SIGNATURE
||"111222| |"'33'"3444| |"555	

Money as Acknowledgment: Remind yourself as you go about your day, that all there is, is a request for appreciation for the services and items you are receiving.

Your I-Have-it List: take a moment today to make a list of everything you have in your life that benefits you – from the clothes you wear, the dollars and cents in your wallet or account, to the dishes in your cupboard, take a moment to take stalk of the abundance already in your experience. Give your attention to what it is you already have. How are you abundant today?

POSITIVE PROJECTION: If you notice your mind projecting a future time of lack, create and use "what if" statements to anticipate abundance.

APPRECIATE! APPRECIATE! APPRECIATE!

::: YOU HAVE MORE THAN ENOUGH OF EVERYTHING FOR TODAY! :::

DAY 3

THOUGHT of the day: Does money feel like freedom or bondage to you? Practice developing a free and relaxed attitude around money. Practice increasing your comfort level with money. Enjoy its function and recognize that it is here only for your enjoyment. Welcome it when it comes into your life, celebrate the having of it when you have it and how ever much of it you have.

Appreciate the dollars that are currently coming into your life. And equally appreciate the money that is leaving your hands since it is leaving in exchange for the services you are receiving. Nothing is ever costing you. "Cost" is a loaded word that says you're losing something. But you're actually gaining something in return for the money you give or pay.

Change your relationship and reactions around the incoming and outgoing flow of dollars. As you change your practiced patterns of thought, you will notice a marked improvement in how you feel about money and the dollars that flow into and out of your life.

PROSPERITY SPREE: Spend your daily cheque from the Universe on new items.

VIBRATING ⊙ ABUNDANCE	
	DATE: _____
PAY TO THE ORDER OF	$18,000
EIGHTEEN THOUSAND	/100 DOLLARS
Universe INC. 444 Abundance Way Billionaire View, CA 000000	*The Universe* AUTHORIZED SIGNATURE
||"111222| |"33"3444| |"555	

Money as Acknowledgment: Remind yourself as you go about your day, that all there is, is a gesture of acknowledgment for the services and items you are receiving. Money is a way of saying "thank you for these services and goods" for everything you are receiving.

Your I-Have-it List: take a moment today to make a list of everything you have in your life that benefits you – from the clothes you wear, the dollars and cents in your wallet or account, to the dishes in your cupboard, take a moment to take stalk of the abundance already in your experience. Give your attention to what it is you already have.

POSITIVE PROJECTION: If you notice your mind projecting a future time of lack, create and use "what if" statements to anticipate abundance.

APPRECIATE! APPRECIATE! APPRECIATE!

::: YOU HAVE MORE THAN ENOUGH OF EVERYTHING FOR TODAY! :::

DAY 4

THOUGHT of the day: Everything you want is already in existence. Everything is energy. Everything is particles in motion. What you conceive of as "money" is no exception. Money, the paper and coin you attribute value to, is nothing more than particles in motion right now appearing before your eyes. It is no different than the table, the chair, your body, or anything else you perceive in this reality. It is your concept of "money" that is actually troublesome to you rather than money itself. It is the power you've practiced giving to "money" that you are now de-constructing through deliberate thinking.

PROSPERITY SPREE: Spend your daily cheque from the Universe on new items.

VIBRATING ⊙ ABUNDANCE		
	DATE: _____	
PAY TO THE ORDER OF	TWENTY TWO THOUSAND	$22,000 /100 DOLLARS
Universe INC. 444 Abundance Way Billionaire View, CA 000000		*The Universe* AUTHORIZED SIGNATURE
	⑈111222⑈ ⑈33⑈3444⑈ ⑈555	

Money as Acknowledgment: Remind yourself as you go about your day, that all there is, is a gesture of acknowledgment for the services and items you are receiving. Money is a way of saying "thank you for these services and goods" for everything you are receiving.

Your I-Have-it List: take a moment today to make a list of everything you have in your life that benefits you – from the clothes you wear, the dollars and cents in your wallet or account, to the dishes in your cupboard, take a moment to take stalk of the abundance already in your experience. Give your attention to what it is you already have.

POSITIVE PROJECTION: If you notice your mind projecting a future time of lack, create and use "what if" statements to anticipate abundance.

APPRECIATE! APPRECIATE! APPRECIATE!

::: YOU HAVE MORE THAN ENOUGH OF EVERYTHING FOR TODAY! :::

DAY 5

THOUGHT of the day: All the money you could ever want is already in existence, for the simple reason that money is nothing more than a form of energy. Just like land. Just like air. Just like water. It is all made up of energy and there is an abundance of it. Think about all the money that is right now in circulation.

There are trillions and trillions of dollars in circulation right in this moment, and the next, and the next. Someone is receiving a cheque for a large sum of money right in this instant. Many someone's are receiving cheques and finding deposits. Many businesses are bringing in large amounts of dollars. Many more are receiving inheritances and gifts. Many are receiving unexpected refunds. Many more are finding coins on their walk. Many are receiving donations. Many are selling their creations. This world that you live in is awash with an endless stream of money. And it's everywhere.

PROSPERITY SPREE: Spend your daily cheque from the Universe on new items.

```
             VIBRATING ⊙ ABUNDANCE
                        DATE: _____
PAY TO THE                        $30,000
ORDER OF
            THIRTY THOUSAND       /100 DOLLARS


Universe INC.
444 Abundance Way                      The Universe
Billionaire View, CA 000000         AUTHORIZED SIGNATURE
                  | |"111222| |"'33'"3444| |"555
```

Money as Acknowledgment: Remind yourself today that there is no such thing as cost, expense, bill, or payment. Whatever you purchase today, whatever your money flows toward, your out-flow is a part of the abundance cycle. Remind yourself as you go about your day, that all there is, is a gesture of acknowledgment for the services and items you are receiving. Money is a way of saying "thank you for these services and goods" for everything you are receiving.

Your I-Have-it List: take a moment today to make a list of everything you have in your life that benefits you – from the clothes you wear, the dollars and cents in your wallet or account, to the dishes in your cupboard, take a moment to take stalk of the abundance already in your experience. Give your attention to what it is you already have.

POSITIVE PROJECTION: If you notice your mind projecting a future time of lack, create and use "what if" statements to anticipate abundance.

APPRECIATE! APPRECIATE! APPRECIATE!

::: YOU HAVE MORE THAN ENOUGH OF EVERYTHING FOR TODAY! :::

DAY 6

THOUGHT of the day: Your idea that there is a limited amount of money stems from your idea of what the source of money is. The source of money is not the outside world. Though you have taught yourself and have been taught to believe this, the only thing that determines how much money comes into your experience is YOU. It's not about the government, or the state of the economy, or your family or anything else. You are the only one who can determine how much money can come into your experience. For the amount of money in your hands or accounts has an exact and direct correlation to your idea of how abundant you are – to the thoughts you entertain and the energy you, in turn, broadcast or emit outward. The money in your life is a materialization of your thoughts about your abundant nature. Expand your idea of how abundant you are, and the abundance in your life will expand in proportion to your inner change.

PROSPERITY SPREE: Spend your daily cheque from the Universe on new items.

```
╔══════════════════════════════════════════════╗
║          VIBRATING ⊙ ABUNDANCE               ║
╚══════════════════════════════════════════════╝
                            DATE: _____
PAY TO THE
ORDER OF                       $40,000
             FORTY THOUSAND    /100 DOLLARS

Universe INC.
444 Abundance Way                  The Universe
Billionaire View, CA 000000     AUTHORIZED SIGNATURE
              | |"111222| |"'33'"3444| |"555
```

Money as Acknowledgment: Remind yourself today that there is no such thing as cost, expense, bill, or payment. Whatever you purchase today, whatever your money flows toward, your out-flow is a part of the abundance cycle. Remind yourself as you go about your day, that all there is, is a gesture of acknowledgment for the services and items you are receiving. Money is a way of saying "thank you for these services and goods" for everything you are receiving.

Your I-Have-it List: take a moment today to make a list of everything you have in your life that benefits you – from the clothes you wear, the dollars and cents in your wallet or account, to the dishes in your cupboard, take a moment to take stalk of the abundance already in your experience. Give your attention to what it is you already have.

POSITIVE PROJECTION: If you notice your mind projecting a future time of lack, create and use "what if" statements to anticipate abundance.

APPRECIATE! APPRECIATE! APPRECIATE!

::: YOU HAVE MORE THAN ENOUGH OF EVERYTHING FOR TODAY! :::

DAY 7

THOUGHT of the day: You are already unlimited in your wealth and have always been. You have always been wealthy. You have always had an endless stream of energy flowing through you and around you, and materializing into your physical experience as your chosen objects. This flow of universal energy does not assert itself into your experience. It comes in exact proportion to your summoning, your asking, your believing, your utilizing, your desiring.

Your concepts or ideas about yourself, your beliefs about yourself and your world, have always been the mold which this limitless flow of energy forms itself around. So as you think in terms of limitation and lack, so does this abundant energy manifest itself as just that. As you change your core beliefs, your blueprints, around money, this abundant energy will begin to form itself around your new template of abundance.

PROSPERITY SPREE: Spend your daily cheque from the Universe on new items.

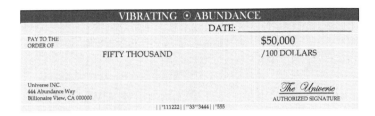

Money as Acknowledgment: Remind yourself today that there is no such thing as cost, expense, bill, or payment. Whatever you purchase today, whatever your money flows toward, your out-flow is a part of the abundance cycle. Remind yourself as you go about your day, that all there is, is a gesture of acknowledgment for the services and items you are receiving. Money is a way of saying "thank you for these services and goods" for everything you are receiving.

Your I-Have-it List: take a moment today to make a list of everything you have in your life that benefits you – from the clothes you wear, the dollars and cents in your wallet or account, to the dishes in your cupboard, take a moment to take stalk of the abundance already in your experience. Give your attention to what it is you already have.

POSITIVE PROJECTION: If you notice your mind projecting a future time of lack, create and use "what if" statements to anticipate abundance.

APPRECIATE! APPRECIATE! APPRECIATE!

::: YOU HAVE MORE THAN ENOUGH OF EVERYTHING FOR TODAY! :::

DAY 8

THOUGHT of the day: You don't have to struggle or work hard to get money. This is only a belief you have practiced. You no more have to struggle to have money than you have to struggle to breathe. It is a natural part of your emergence into this reality. Abundance is yours because you exist. Money is a given simply because you exist. It is only your practiced expectation that interferes with the manifestation of your natural abundance.

PROSPERITY SPREE: Spend your daily cheque from the Universe on new items.

VIBRATING ⊙ ABUNDANCE	
	DATE. _____
PAY TO THE ORDER OF _____ SIXTY THOUSAND	$60,000 /100 DOLLARS
Universe INC. 444 Abundance Way Billionaire View, CA 000000	*The Universe* AUTHORIZED SIGNATURE
||"111222||"33"'3444||"555	

Money as Acknowledgment: Remind yourself today that there is no such thing as cost, expense, bill, or payment. Whatever you purchase today, whatever your money flows toward, your out-flow is a part of the abundance cycle. Remind yourself as you go about your day, that all there is, is a gesture of acknowledgment for the services and items you are receiving. Money is a way of saying "thank you for these services and goods" for everything you are receiving.

Your I-Have-it List: take a moment today to make a list of everything you have in your life that benefits you – from the clothes you wear, the dollars and cents in your wallet or account, to the dishes in your cupboard, take a moment to take stalk of the abundance already in your experience. Give your attention to what it is you already have.

POSITIVE PROJECTION: If you notice your mind projecting a future time of lack, create and use "what if" statements to anticipate abundance.

APPRECIATE! APPRECIATE! APPRECIATE!

::: YOU HAVE MORE THAN ENOUGH OF EVERYTHING FOR TODAY! :::

DAY 9

THOUGHT of the day: There is no shortage in this Universe. There is not a single thing that is running out. There is not a single thing that there is "not enough" of. These experiences of lack or shortage or limitation are all manifestations of human thinking of scarcity – scarcity consciousness. Universal energy forms itself exactly in accord with your thoughts and beliefs. There is no other builder. There is no other molder of this universal energy. So as you begin to think in terms of abundance, the reality of your own natural abundance will materialize before your eyes. It is facing you even now as you read these words. Everything you see materialized as the objects in your world right now is the endless abundance of this Universe showing itself to you in the likeness of your dominant thought-waves. Put your attention on this abundance and it will expand in your life.

PROSPERITY SPREE: Spend your daily cheque from the Universe on new items.

```
╔══════════════════════════════════════════════════╗
              VIBRATING ⊙ ABUNDANCE
                             DATE: _____
  PAY TO THE                      $75,000
  ORDER OF
              SEVENTY FIVE THOUSAND   /100 DOLLARS


  Universe INC.
  444 Abundance Way                    The Universe
  Billionaire View, CA 000000       AUTHORIZED SIGNATURE
              |｜"111222｜｜"33"'3444｜｜"555
╚══════════════════════════════════════════════════╝
```

Money as Acknowledgment: Remind yourself today that there is no such thing as cost, expense, bill, or payment. Whatever you purchase today, whatever your money flows toward, your out-flow is a part of the abundance cycle. Remind yourself as you go about your day, that all there is, is a gesture of acknowledgment for the services and items you are receiving. Money is a way of saying "thank you for these services and goods" for everything you are receiving.

Your I-Have-it List: take a moment today to make a list of everything you have in your life that benefits you – from the clothes you wear, the dollars and cents in your wallet or account, to the dishes in your cupboard, take a moment to take stalk of the abundance already in your experience. Give your attention to what it is you already have.

POSITIVE PROJECTION: If you notice your mind projecting a future time of lack, create and use "what if" statements to anticipate abundance.

APPRECIATE! APPRECIATE! APPRECIATE!

::: YOU HAVE MORE THAN ENOUGH OF EVERYTHING FOR TODAY! :::

DAY 10

THOUGHT of the day: Appreciating what has manifested right now into your experience is the quickest way to get yourself into receiving mode. Appreciation is a higher vibration. Thoughts of appreciation are vibrating at a higher frequency. That's why it always feels good to give and receive appreciation. Your body translates all higher frequencies as good feelings.

So the more you appreciate in your daily experience, the more you appreciate the things that have come in response to your asking (because everything in your reality right now is there only because of the thoughts you have thought), you open yourself up even more to allow Universal Energy to flow through you and to you in the likeness of the things you've asked for.

THANKING WHAT YOU DO HAVE RIGHT NOW: "I so appreciate the money I have now. I so appreciate that the money I have has come in response to my thoughts. I so appreciate everything that I have right now. I so appreciate my home, my bed, my furniture, and everything else that has come into my experience. I so appreciate all the services I receive. I so appreciate that I have heating. I so appreciate that I have air conditioning. I so appreciate that I have a car that gets me everywhere. I so appreciate that I have public transportation. I so appreciate that I have more than enough of everything to meet my needs for today."

PROSPERITY SPREE: Spend your daily cheque from the Universe on new items.

VIBRATING ⊙ ABUNDANCE	
DATE: _____	
PAY TO THE ORDER OF	$80,000
EIGHTY THOUSAND	/100 DOLLARS
Universe INC. 444 Abundance Way Billionaire View, CA 000000	*The Universe* AUTHORIZED SIGNATURE
⑈"111222⑈ ⑈"33"'3444⑈ ⑈"555	

Money as Acknowledgment: Remind yourself today that there is no such thing as cost, expense, bill, or payment. Whatever you purchase today, whatever your money flows toward, your out-flow is a part of the abundance cycle. Remind yourself as you go about your day, that all there is, is a gesture of acknowledgment for the services and items you are receiving. Money is a way of saying "thank you for these services and goods" for everything you are receiving.

Your I-Have-it List: take a moment today to make a list of everything you have in your life that benefits you – from the clothes you wear, the dollars and cents in your wallet or account, to the dishes in your cupboard, take a moment to take stalk of the abundance already in your experience. Give your attention to what it is you already have.

POSITIVE PROJECTION: If you notice your mind projecting a future time of lack, create and use "what if" statements to anticipate abundance.

APPRECIATE! APPRECIATE! APPRECIATE!

::: YOU HAVE MORE THAN ENOUGH OF EVERYTHING FOR TODAY! :::

DAY 11

THOUGHT of the day: There is absolutely MORE than enough of everything for everyone. There is no shortage of energy. There is no shortage of universal energy. There is more than enough for everyone. No one is taking more than their share and no one is getting less than their share. Every being receives as much as their concepts, their expectations and ideas, allow them to receive. The only thing that determines how much of anything comes into your experience is your own beliefs – that's all. The actual supply is endless and unlimited. Your source and resource for all things is Infinite and Unfailing Abundance.

PROSPERITY SPREE: Spend your daily cheque from the Universe on new items.

```
         VIBRATING ⊙ ABUNDANCE
                      DATE: _____
PAY TO THE
ORDER OF                            $90,000
             NINTY THOUSAND         /100 DOLLARS

Universe INC.
444 Abundance Way                     The Universe
Billionaire View, CA 000000         AUTHORIZED SIGNATURE
                  ||"111222||"'33"'3444||"555
```

Money as Acknowledgment: Remind yourself today that there is no such thing as cost, expense, bill, or payment. Whatever you purchase today, whatever your money flows toward, your out-flow is a part of the abundance cycle. Remind yourself as you go about your day, that all there is, is a gesture of acknowledgment for the services and items you are receiving. Money is a way of saying "thank you for these services and goods" for everything you are receiving.

Your I-Have-it List: take a moment today to make a list of everything you have in your life that benefits you – from the clothes you wear, the dollars and cents in your wallet or account, to the dishes in your cupboard, take a moment to take stalk of the abundance already in your experience. Give your attention to what it is you already have.

POSITIVE PROJECTION: If you notice your mind projecting a future time of lack, create and use "what if" statements to anticipate abundance.

APPRECIATE! APPRECIATE! APPRECIATE!

::: YOU HAVE MORE THAN ENOUGH OF EVERYTHING FOR TODAY! :::

DAY 12

THOUGHT of the day: You don't get agitated and feel lack-full when you exhale, when you release the air from your lungs. When you breathe out, you don't feel like you're losing something. You naturally and innately let air in and out of your being without thought as to if there's going to be more air or if there's going to be enough air later. You trust in the infinite supply of oxygen. Bring yourself to trust in the infinite supply of the energy that comes as money into your experience. As you let go of the not enough-ness thoughts you've practiced, money will easily flow into your life in so many expected and unexpected ways.

PROSPERITY SPREE: Spend your daily cheque from the Universe on new items.

VIBRATING ⊙ ABUNDANCE

DATE: _____

PAY TO THE ORDER OF _____

ONE HUNDRED THOUSAND $100,000 /100 DOLLARS

Universe INC.
444 Abundance Way
Billionaire View, CA 000000

The Universe
AUTHORIZED SIGNATURE

| |"111222| |"'33"'3444| |"555

Money as Acknowledgment: Remind yourself today that there is no such thing as cost, expense, bill, or payment. Whatever you purchase today, whatever your money flows toward, your out-flow is a part of the abundance cycle. Remind yourself as you go about your day, that all there is, is a gesture of acknowledgment for the services and items you are receiving. Money is a way of saying "thank you for these services and goods" for everything you are receiving.

Your I-Have-it List: take a moment today to make a list of everything you have in your life that benefits you – from the clothes you wear, the dollars and cents in your wallet or account, to the dishes in your cupboard, take a moment to take stalk of the abundance already in your experience. Give your attention to what it is you already have.

POSITIVE PROJECTION: If you notice your mind projecting a future time of lack, create and use "what if" statements to anticipate abundance.

APPRECIATE! APPRECIATE! APPRECIATE!

::: YOU HAVE MORE THAN ENOUGH OF EVERYTHING FOR TODAY! :::

DAY 13

THOUGHT of the day: Practice thoughts like "there is always more coming" "my source of abundance is unlimited and unending". With every positive thought you repeatedly entertain you expand or add to your consciousness – you expand your ability to ask & receive. A wealth consciousness is nothing more than the consciousness of someone who has solidified thoughts of prosperity and abundance in their own mind. And this is something you are right now doing deliberately.

PROSPERITY SPREE: Spend your daily cheque from the Universe on new items.

VIBRATING ⊙ ABUNDANCE	
DATE: _____	
PAY TO THE ORDER OF ONE HUNDRED TWENTY FIVE THOUSAND	$125,000 /100 DOLLARS
Universe INC. 444 Abundance Way Billionaire View, CA 000000	*The Universe* AUTHORIZED SIGNATURE
ǀǀ"111222ǀǀ'"33'"3444ǀǀ"555	

Money as Acknowledgment: Remind yourself today that there is no such thing as cost, expense, bill, or payment. Whatever you purchase today, whatever your money flows toward, your out-flow is a part of the abundance cycle. Remind yourself as you go about your day, that all there is, is a gesture of acknowledgment for the services and items you are receiving. Money is a way of saying "thank you for these services and goods" for everything you are receiving.

Your I-Have-it List: take a moment today to make a list of everything you have in your life that benefits you – from the clothes you wear, the dollars and cents in your wallet or account, to the dishes in your cupboard, take a moment to take stalk of the abundance already in your experience. Give your attention to what it is you already have.

POSITIVE PROJECTION: If you notice your mind projecting a future time of lack, create and use "what if" statements to anticipate abundance.

APPRECIATE! APPRECIATE! APPRECIATE!

::: YOU HAVE MORE THAN ENOUGH OF EVERYTHING FOR TODAY! :::

DAY 14

THOUGHT of the day: How you feel when you receive a bill or bank statement is a good indicator of the balance of your thoughts on the subject of money. If the "outgoing" money is a negative experience for you, this is indicating to you your belief in shortage. The outflow of money is part of the abundance cycle. Just like air moves in and out of your lungs without ever diminishing or depleting the air supply of your world, so does the abundance cycle work in the same way. Practice seeing the outflow of money as something that's just opening you up so that more money can come in. Bring yourself into the knowing that the outflow of money is in no way depleting your supply. There is always more coming.

PROSPERITY SPREE: Spend your daily cheque from the Universe on new items.

VIBRATING ⊙ ABUNDANCE	
DATE: _____	
PAY TO THE ORDER OF ONE HUNDRED FIFTY THOUSAND	$150,000 /100 DOLLARS
Universe INC. 444 Abundance Way Billionaire View, CA 000000	*The Universe* AUTHORIZED SIGNATURE
||"111222||"'33'"3444||"555	

Money as Acknowledgment: Remind yourself today that there is no such thing as cost, expense, bill, or payment. Whatever you purchase today, whatever your money flows toward, your out-flow is a part of the abundance cycle. Remind yourself as you go about your day, that all there is, is a gesture of acknowledgment for the services and items you are receiving. Money is a way of saying "thank you for these services and goods" for everything you are receiving.

Your I-Have-it List: take a moment today to make a list of everything you have in your life that benefits you – from the clothes you wear, the dollars and cents in your wallet or account, to the dishes in your cupboard, take a moment to take stalk of the abundance already in your experience. Give your attention to what it is you already have.

POSITIVE PROJECTION: If you notice your mind projecting a future time of lack, create and use "what if" statements to anticipate abundance.

APPRECIATE! APPRECIATE! APPRECIATE!

::: YOU HAVE MORE THAN ENOUGH OF EVERYTHING FOR TODAY! :::

DAY 15

THOUGHT of the day: Resisting or experiencing negative emotion over outgoing money only arises from a perspective of "I'm going to run out" or "there isn't enough". There is an ebb and flow to everything in existence, to everything in this energetic environment. Everything is moving into and out of something. It is a cycle, a give and take type of relationship formed between every aspect of this reality.

Money is no different to this natural rhythm. Money, like all things made of energy, needs to flow in and out of your experience to keep to the natural and expanding rhythm of this life. You're not meant to hoard money any more than you are meant to suck in all the air and never exhale again.

Practice thinking of the outgoing money, the payments and purchases or unexpected spending, as part of the natural rhythm of all life. The more ease you have over what goes out, the more you're open to receive. Come to recognize any type of resistance or feeling of constraint in spending money is coming from scarcity consciousness. There is nothing scarce about the abundance of this Universe. Money is no exception.

PROSPERITY SPREE: Spend your daily cheque from the Universe on new items.

VIBRATING ⊙ ABUNDANCE	
	DATE: _____
PAY TO THE ORDER OF _____ TWO HUNDRED THOUSAND	$200,000 /100 DOLLARS
Universe INC. 444 Abundance Way Billionaire View, CA 000000	*The Universe* AUTHORIZED SIGNATURE
	⎪⎪"111222⎪⎪"'33'"3444⎪⎪"555

Money as Acknowledgment: Remind yourself today that there is no such thing as cost, expense, bill, or payment. Whatever you purchase today, whatever your money flows toward, your out-flow is a part of the abundance cycle. Remind yourself as you go about your day, that all there is, is a gesture of acknowledgment for the services and items you are receiving. Money is a way of saying "thank you for these services and goods" for everything you are receiving.

Your I-Have-it List: take a moment today to make a list of everything you have in your life that benefits you – from the clothes you wear, the dollars and cents in your wallet or account, to the dishes in your cupboard, take a moment to take stalk of the abundance already in your experience. Give your attention to what it is you already have.

POSITIVE PROJECTION: If you notice

your mind projecting a future time of lack, create and use "what if" statements to anticipate abundance.

APPRECIATE! APPRECIATE! APPRECIATE!

::: YOU HAVE MORE THAN ENOUGH OF EVERYTHING FOR TODAY! :::

DAY 16

THOUGHT of the day: What does having money feel like? What does having an abundance of dollars feel like? Freedom. Feel that. Think about what it feels like to have all the money you have ever dreamed of. What do you see yourself doing? What are you feeling while you're doing these things with all this money?
That feeling of having money, that sense of freedom and ease, is the vibration you want to achieve within yourself. Deliberately match the vibration of having money by practicing better feeling thoughts on abundance, wealth, and prosperity. As you expand your wealth consciousness deliberately, you are and will magnetize abundance of all types toward you. Focus on the things that right now generate the feelings of freedom and joy within you. Rest your attention on these things. Give them more of your attention. The more you generate the feelings of freedom and joy within yourself, the more you radiate these frequencies outward – and the energy you radiate will always translate into a physical experience that evokes more of that frequency in you.

PROSPERITY SPREE: Spend your daily cheque from the Universe on new items.

```
         VIBRATING ⊙ ABUNDANCE
                         DATE: _____
PAY TO THE
ORDER OF                                $300,000
              THREE HUNDRED THOUSAND    /100 DOLLARS


Universe INC.
444 Abundance Way                        The Universe
Billionaire View, CA 000000              AUTHORIZED SIGNATURE
              | |"111222| |"'33"'3444| |"555
```

Money as Acknowledgment: Remind yourself today that there is no such thing as cost, expense, bill, or payment. Whatever you purchase today, whatever your money flows toward, your out-flow is a part of the abundance cycle. Remind yourself as you go about your day, that all there is, is a gesture of acknowledgment for the services and items you are receiving. Money is a way of saying "thank you for these services and goods" for everything you are receiving.

Your I-Have-it List: take a moment today to make a list of everything you have in your life that benefits you – from the clothes you wear, the dollars and cents in your wallet or account, to the dishes in your cupboard, take a moment to take stalk of the abundance already in your experience. Give your attention to what it is you already have.

POSITIVE PROJECTION: If you notice your mind projecting a future time of lack, create and use "what if" statements to anticipate abundance.

APPRECIATE! APPRECIATE! APPRECIATE!

::: YOU HAVE MORE THAN ENOUGH OF EVERYTHING FOR TODAY! :::

DAY 17

THOUGHT of the day: Being abundance-minded is really about recognizing how wealthy you have always been. When every single thing in the universe is made of energy, when everything is energy, what are you really cut off from?

There is an endless stream of positive energy flowing to you and through you in every moment. It never ceases. It is constantly and endlessly flowing toward you and through you. The resources of the entire Universe are available to you at all times, and money is just one small materialization of these infinite resources. You've always had wealth, and as you come to recognize that, your ability to materialize it into your physical experience will astonish you.

PROSPERITY SPREE: Spend your daily cheque from the Universe on new items.

VIBRATING ⊙ ABUNDANCE	
DATE: _____	
PAY TO THE ORDER OF FOUR HUNDRED THOUSAND	$400,000 /100 DOLLARS
Universe INC. 444 Abundance Way Billionaire View, CA 000000	*The Universe* AUTHORIZED SIGNATURE
||"111222||"'33'"3444||"555	

Money as Acknowledgment: Remind

yourself today that there is no such thing as cost, expense, bill, or payment. Whatever you purchase today, whatever your money flows toward, your out-flow is a part of the abundance cycle. Remind yourself as you go about your day, that all there is, is a gesture of acknowledgment for the services and items you are receiving. Money is a way of saying "thank you for these services and goods" for everything you are receiving.

Your I-Have-it List: take a moment today to make a list of everything you have in your life that benefits you – from the clothes you wear, the dollars and cents in your wallet or account, to the dishes in your cupboard, take a moment to take stalk of the abundance already in your experience. Give your attention to what it is you already have.

POSITIVE PROJECTION: If you notice your mind projecting a future time of lack, create and use "what if" statements to anticipate abundance.

APPRECIATE! APPRECIATE! APPRECIATE!

::: YOU HAVE MORE THAN ENOUGH OF EVERYTHING FOR TODAY! :::

DAY 18

THOUGHT of the day: Like all things in this life, money flourishes under the conditions of appreciation and love. The higher vibrations of appreciation and love carry the most magnetic attractive force in this experience. Love and appreciate the money you already have.

Every cent and every dollar has materialized into your experience in accord with your wealth consciousness, and it is what you do have right now that's allowing you to experience the kinds of things you are experiencing. The money in your purse, wallet, or account has materialized just for you. Loving and appreciating money, the inflow and outflow of it, is the fastest way to attract more of it into your experience.

Recognize that by practicing appreciating what it is that you do have, you are training yourself to be in the very vibration that will give you more of what you want.

PROSPERITY SPREE: Spend your daily cheque from the Universe on new items.

```
┌─────────────────────────────────────────────────────────┐
│            VIBRATING ⊙ ABUNDANCE                        │
│                       DATE: _____             │
│  PAY TO THE                                             │
│  ORDER OF                        $500,000               │
│           FIVE HUNDRED THOUSAND  /100 DOLLARS           │
│                                                         │
│  Universe INC.                                          │
│  444 Abundance Way               The Universe           │
│  Billionaire View, CA 000000     AUTHORIZED SIGNATURE   │
│              ||"111222||"33"3444||"555                  │
└─────────────────────────────────────────────────────────┘

**Money as Acknowledgment**: Remind yourself today that there is no such thing as cost, expense, bill, or payment. Whatever you purchase today, whatever your money flows toward, your out-flow is a part of the abundance cycle. Remind yourself as you go about your day, that all there is, is a gesture of acknowledgment for the services and items you are receiving. Money is a way of saying "thank you for these services and goods" for everything you are receiving.

**Your I-Have-it List:** take a moment today to make a list of everything you have in your life that benefits you – from the clothes you wear, the dollars and cents in your wallet or account, to the dishes in your cupboard, take a moment to take stalk of the abundance already in your experience. Give your attention to what it is you already have.

**POSITIVE PROJECTION**: If you notice your mind projecting a future time of lack, create and use "what if" statements to anticipate abundance.
```

APPRECIATE! APPRECIATE! APPRECIATE!

::: YOU HAVE MORE THAN ENOUGH OF EVERYTHING FOR TODAY! :::

DAY 19

THOUGHT of the day: Any kind of resistance you experience toward and around money, whether it is fear of running out or something else, any kind of negative emotion is indicating to you that in that moment you are resisting the flow of dollars in your experience. Your practiced negativity, your scarcity consciousness, is the only thing that repels the influx of dollars.

There is nothing outside of you determining what you can or can't have. The only thing that determines what flows into your experience is your own habit of thought, your practiced vibration, and the actions that stem from that. There is nothing that is outside of your hands. It all revolves around you and your practiced or habituated vibrational pattern. You have more control over what comes to you than you realize.

PROSPERITY SPREE: Spend your daily cheque from the Universe on new items.

VIBRATING ⊙ ABUNDANCE	
	DATE: _____
PAY TO THE ORDER OF SIX HUNDRED THOUSAND	$600,000 /100 DOLLARS
Universe INC. 444 Abundance Way Billionaire View, CA 000000	*The Universe* AUTHORIZED SIGNATURE

Money as Acknowledgment: Remind yourself today that there is no such thing as cost, expense, bill, or payment. Whatever you purchase today, whatever your money flows toward, your out-flow is a part of the abundance cycle. Remind yourself as you go about your day, that all there is, is a gesture of acknowledgment for the services and items you are receiving. Money is a way of saying "thank you for these services and goods" for everything you are receiving.

Your I-Have-it List: take a moment today to make a list of everything you have in your life that benefits you – from the clothes you wear, the dollars and cents in your wallet or account, to the dishes in your cupboard, take a moment to take stalk of the abundance already in your experience. Give your attention to what it is you already have.

POSITIVE PROJECTION: If you notice your mind projecting a future time of lack, create and use "what if" statements to anticipate abundance.

APPRECIATE! APPRECIATE! APPRECIATE!

::: YOU HAVE MORE THAN ENOUGH OF EVERYTHING FOR TODAY! :::

DAY 20

THOUGHT of the day: There is nothing that is good or bad about money. Money is just colored paper, or an arrangement of numbers that appear in your accounts and on your bill statements. Think about that. Examine your ideas and practiced beliefs around money. Think about the cliché's you've heard. Cliché's like "money is the root of all evil" or the undercurrent or silent assumption that wealth is for the few.

All of these come from scarcity consciousness. When everything is made up of energy, of particles that are vibrating constantly, when everything in this entire universe is just energy, what is this negativity really pointing to? How is it one form of energy such as a tree is considered "good" and another form of this same energy like money considered "evil"? The only struggle you ever have is with your own ideas about something. The thing itself is void of any meaning as every single thing is made up of the same neutral substance.

What meaning have you given to the having of money? What ideas have you inherited from your environment and incorporated into your root beliefs on the subject of money?

PROSPERITY SPREE: Spend your daily cheque from the Universe on new items.

```
┌─────────────────────────────────────────────────┐
│          VIBRATING ⊙ ABUNDANCE                  │
│                         DATE: _____           │
│  PAY TO THE                                     │
│  ORDER OF                         $700,000      │
│         SEVEN HUNDRED THOUSAND    /100 DOLLARS  │
│                                                 │
│  Universe INC.                                  │
│  444 Abundance Way                The Universe  │
│  Billionaire View, CA 000000    AUTHORIZED SIGNATURE │
│              ||"111222||"'33'"3444||"555        │
└─────────────────────────────────────────────────┘
```

Money as Acknowledgment: Remind yourself today that there is no such thing as cost, expense, bill, or payment. Whatever you purchase today, whatever your money flows toward, your out-flow is a part of the abundance cycle. Remind yourself as you go about your day, that all there is, is a gesture of acknowledgment for the services and items you are receiving. Money is a way of saying "thank you for these services and goods" for everything you are receiving.

Your I-Have-it List: take a moment today to make a list of everything you have in your life that benefits you – from the clothes you wear, the dollars and cents in your wallet or account, to the dishes in your cupboard, take a moment to take stalk of the abundance already in your experience. Give your attention to what it is you already have.

POSITIVE PROJECTION: If you notice

your mind projecting a future time of lack, create and use "what if" statements to anticipate abundance.

APPRECIATE! APPRECIATE! APPRECIATE!

::: YOU HAVE MORE THAN ENOUGH OF EVERYTHING FOR TODAY! :::

DAY 21

THOUGHT of the day: It is through the exchange of money for services that you access avenues of life that you may not otherwise access. It is the exchange of money for a seat on an airplane to a destination you've never been to, that allows you to get to that destination and experience it.

The money you put into your environment through "paying" for services isn't just leaving your hand. It's going into someone else's hand. It's going to feed someone else. It's going to cloth someone else. It's going to buy someone else some needed or desired thing.

Allow yourself to see the reach of the dollars that leave your hands and recognize that you're not losing anything. You are providing for someone else while at the same time receiving your desired service. You are a part of the chain of abundance in this experience. Train yourself to see your out-flow in this way.

PROSPERITY SPREE: Spend your daily cheque from the Universe on new items.

```
╔════════════════════════════════════════════════╗
║         VIBRATING ⊙ ABUNDANCE                  ║
║                         DATE: _____  ║
║  PAY TO THE                                    ║
║  ORDER OF                      $800,000        ║
║         EIGHT HUNDRED THOUSAND /100 DOLLARS    ║
║                                                ║
║  Universe INC.                                 ║
║  444 Abundance Way            The Universe     ║
║  Billionaire View, CA 000000  AUTHORIZED SIGNATURE ║
║           |∣"111222∣∣"'33'"3444∣∣"555           ║
╚════════════════════════════════════════════════╝
```

Money as Acknowledgment: Remind yourself today that there is no such thing as cost, expense, bill, or payment. Whatever you purchase today, whatever your money flows toward, your out-flow is a part of the abundance cycle. Remind yourself as you go about your day, that all there is, is a gesture of acknowledgment for the services and items you are receiving. Money is a way of saying "thank you for these services and goods" for everything you are receiving.

Your I-Have-it List: take a moment today to make a list of everything you have in your life that benefits you – from the clothes you wear, the dollars and cents in your wallet or account, to the dishes in your cupboard, take a moment to take stalk of the abundance already in your experience. Give your attention to what it is you already have.

POSITIVE PROJECTION: If you notice your mind projecting a future time of lack, create and use "what if" statements to anticipate abundance.

APPRECIATE! APPRECIATE! APPRECIATE!

::: YOU HAVE MORE THAN ENOUGH OF EVERYTHING FOR TODAY! :::

DAY 22

THOUGHT of the day: The Universe can only reciprocate the energy or vibration you radiate. You are always on a continuous feedback loop with the Unified Field, or the Universe which you are an integrated part of.

Whatever you radiate through your thoughts and beliefs around money is what you get back. If you radiate fear and anxiety around money, then you will materialize endless situations that continue to perpetuate those kinds of feelings in you.

The Universe cannot assert abundance on you. The Field cannot impose prosperity onto you. You must begin to radiate these energies, by deliberately developing your wealth consciousness so that the feedback you get from the Universe as the situations of your daily experiences can be as you want them to be.

PROSPERITY SPREE: Spend your daily cheque from the Universe on new items.

```
           VIBRATING ⊙ ABUNDANCE
                         DATE: _____
PAY TO THE
ORDER OF                          $900,000
            NINE HUNDRED THOUSAND /100 DOLLARS

Universe INC.
444 Abundance Way
Billionaire View, CA 000000           The Universe
                                   AUTHORIZED SIGNATURE
           | |"111222| |'"33"'3444| |"555
```

Money as Acknowledgment: Remind yourself today that there is no such thing as cost, expense, bill, or payment. Whatever you purchase today, whatever your money flows toward, your out-flow is a part of the abundance cycle. Remind yourself as you go about your day, that all there is, is a gesture of acknowledgment for the services and items you are receiving. Money is a way of saying "thank you for these services and goods" for everything you are receiving.

Your I-Have-it List: take a moment today to make a list of everything you have in your life that benefits you – from the clothes you wear, the dollars and cents in your wallet or account, to the dishes in your cupboard, take a moment to take stalk of the abundance already in your experience. Give your attention to what it is you already have.

POSITIVE PROJECTION: If you notice your mind projecting a future time of lack, create and use "what if" statements to anticipate abundance.

APPRECIATE! APPRECIATE! APPRECIATE!

::: YOU HAVE MORE THAN ENOUGH OF EVERYTHING FOR TODAY! :::

DAY 23

THOUGHT of the day: When you see money as something apart and isolated from you, you run the risk of seeing it as negative, unnecessary, or even evil and bad. But money is not apart from you. It is a part of the energy stream that animates all of life and this reality. It is made of the very substance that the ocean and the earth are made of. It is energy undeniably and without a doubt, and so it is an extension of everything that you are.

Your oneness with money can come to be an idea you don't shrug away from or cringe over. Let go of the negativity you've collected around the subject of money. Let go of your inherited assumptions about what money is. See that it is a part of this reality as much as anything else you value and praise. Money is an extension of you and your ideas about yourself. The only thing that is keeping money away from you are your limited ideas of it and of your abundance. You are the only one who can allow or restrict the flow of dollars into your experience and you are the only one that can change your relationship with money.

You've always been infinitely abundant, as you see that, your reality will shift to mirror that. Know it and you will live it.

PROSPERITY SPREE: Spend your daily cheque from the Universe on new items.

```
        VIBRATING ⊙ ABUNDANCE
                        DATE: _____
PAY TO THE
ORDER OF                       $1,000,000
               ONE MILLION     /100 DOLLARS

Universe INC.
444 Abundance Way                 The Universe
Billionaire View, CA 000000    AUTHORIZED SIGNATURE
        | |"111222| |"'33'"3444| |"555
```

Money as Acknowledgment: Remind yourself today that there is no such thing as cost, expense, bill, or payment. Whatever you purchase today, whatever your money flows toward, your out-flow is a part of the abundance cycle. Remind yourself as you go about your day, that all there is, is a gesture of acknowledgment for the services and items you are receiving. Money is a way of saying "thank you for these services and goods" for everything you are receiving.

Your I-Have-it List: take a moment today to make a list of everything you have in your life that benefits you – from the clothes you wear, the dollars and cents in your wallet or account, to the dishes in your cupboard, take a moment to take stalk of the abundance already in your experience. Give your attention to what it is you already have.

POSITIVE PROJECTION: If you notice

your mind projecting a future time of lack, create and use "what if" statements to anticipate abundance.

APPRECIATE! APPRECIATE! APPRECIATE!

::: YOU HAVE MORE THAN ENOUGH OF EVERYTHING FOR TODAY! :::

DAY 24

THOUGHT of the day: Open your eyes to the natural abundance of the Universe. Be determined to see just how lavishing life is. The abundance of oceans, the abundance of air, the abundance of earth, the abundance of space, the abundance of species, and the abundance of living and non-living things is all around you. Look at your immediate environment and see just how much "stuff" there is all around you. Furniture and books, clothes and buildings, food of all kinds, endless variety of seeds and stars, factories and everything else you can imagine – it is all in front of you in abundance. Focus on this. Focus on just how there is "too much" of everything all around you. This is the way of the Universe, to supply in outrageous abundance.

In a Universe of excess, what is there to limit the excess of dollars in your life?

PROSPERITY SPREE: Spend your daily cheque from the Universe on new items.

VIBRATING ⊙ ABUNDANCE	
DATE: _____	
PAY TO THE ORDER OF _____ TWO MILLION	$2,000,000 /100 DOLLARS
Universe INC. 444 Abundance Way Billionaire View, CA 000000	*The Universe* AUTHORIZED SIGNATURE
⑈"111222⑈ ⑈"33"'3444⑈ ⑈"555	

Money as Acknowledgment: Remind yourself today that there is no such thing as cost, expense, bill, or payment. Whatever you purchase today, whatever your money flows toward, your out-flow is a part of the abundance cycle. Remind yourself as you go about your day, that all there is, is a gesture of acknowledgment for the services and items you are receiving. Money is a way of saying "thank you for these services and goods" for everything you are receiving.

Your I-Have-it List: take a moment today to make a list of everything you have in your life that benefits you – from the clothes you wear, the dollars and cents in your wallet or account, to the dishes in your cupboard, take a moment to take stalk of the abundance already in your experience. Give your attention to what it is you already have.

POSITIVE PROJECTION: If you notice your mind projecting a future time of lack, create and use "what if" statements to anticipate abundance.

APPRECIATE! APPRECIATE! APPRECIATE!

::: YOU HAVE MORE THAN ENOUGH OF EVERYTHING FOR TODAY! :::

DAY 25

THOUGHT of the day: To the extent that you believe in shortage and scarcity, to the extent that you anchor scarcity consciousness within yourself, to the extent you practice thoughts that say "there isn't enough" or "I'm going to run out", you will materialize situations and circumstances that mirror the essence of these thoughts. Your thoughts are at the root of everything you experience. So when your practiced pattern of thought, your beliefs, are recognizing the natural abundance of everything that you are, this will be your experience in all avenues of your life.

PROSPERITY SPREE: Spend your daily cheque from the Universe on new items.

VIBRATING ⊙ ABUNDANCE	
	DATE: _____
PAY TO THE ORDER OF THREE MILLION	$3,000,000 /100 DOLLARS
Universe INC. 444 Abundance Way Billionaire View, CA 000000	*The Universe* AUTHORIZED SIGNATURE
⎪⎪ ⁚111222⎪ ⎪ ⁚⁚33⁚⁚3444⎪ ⎪ ⁚555	

Money as Acknowledgment: Remind yourself today that there is no such thing as cost, expense, bill, or payment. Whatever you purchase today, whatever your money flows toward, your out-flow is a part of the abundance cycle. Remind yourself as you go about your day, that all there is, is a gesture of acknowledgment for the services and items you are receiving. Money is a way of saying "thank you for these services and goods" for everything you are receiving.

Your I-Have-it List: take a moment today to make a list of everything you have in your life that benefits you – from the clothes you wear, the dollars and cents in your wallet or account, to the dishes in your cupboard, take a moment to take stalk of the abundance already in your experience. Give your attention to what it is you already have.

POSITIVE PROJECTION: If you notice your mind projecting a future time of lack, create and use "what if" statements to anticipate abundance.

APPRECIATE! APPRECIATE! APPRECIATE!

::: YOU HAVE MORE THAN ENOUGH OF EVERYTHING FOR TODAY! :::

DAY 26

THOUGHT of the day: Wealth isn't about hard work and having multiple jobs or working 80 hours weekly in a place you don't enjoy, to amass dollars. Wealth, the kind that lasts, is first and foremost a state of mind that then materializes as abundance and prosperity in your life in inspired and creative ways.

It is rooted in your being, in who you are and who you see yourself to be. Abundance is your birthright and natural state of being. You are an offspring of pure and infinite abundance. You are made of the very abundant substance that everything else is made of – infinite and intelligent energy. There is a wealth of information on what this reality is. There is a wealth of information on what wealth itself is. There is an abundance of information on expanding your wealth consciousness right now in your environment. Build your wealth from the inside out. Change your practiced thoughts first and expand your abundance consciousness. Everything else extends out from there.

PROSPERITY SPREE: Spend your daily cheque from the Universe on new items.

```
╔══════════════════════════════════════════════════╗
║        VIBRATING ⊙ ABUNDANCE                     ║
║                         DATE: _____  ║
║ PAY TO THE                                       ║
║ ORDER OF                          $4,000,000     ║
║              FOUR MILLION         /100 DOLLARS   ║
║                                                  ║
║ Universe INC.                                    ║
║ 444 Abundance Way                   The Universe ║
║ Billionaire View, CA 000000      AUTHORIZED SIGNATURE ║
║          | |"111222| |"'33'"3444| |"555          ║
╚══════════════════════════════════════════════════╝
```

Money as Acknowledgment: Remind yourself today that there is no such thing as cost, expense, bill, or payment. Whatever you purchase today, whatever your money flows toward, your out-flow is a part of the abundance cycle. Remind yourself as you go about your day, that all there is, is a gesture of acknowledgment for the services and items you are receiving. Money is a way of saying "thank you for these services and goods" for everything you are receiving.

Your I-Have-it List: take a moment today to make a list of everything you have in your life that benefits you – from the clothes you wear, the dollars and cents in your wallet or account, to the dishes in your cupboard, take a moment to take stalk of the abundance already in your experience. Give your attention to what it is you already have.

POSITIVE PROJECTION: If you notice your mind projecting a future time of lack, create and use "what if" statements to anticipate abundance.

APPRECIATE! APPRECIATE! APPRECIATE!

::: YOU HAVE MORE THAN ENOUGH OF EVERYTHING FOR TODAY! :::

DAY 27

THOUGHT of the day: Money is not your supply, your support, your security, or your safety. Your consciousness, your dominant pattern of thought is where everything you have, has materialized from. The outside is not your source of supply. The outside world is not your source of anything. The outside world is only reflecting or mirroring your dominant internal state – your dominant vibrational balance. Everything that comes into your experience is coming in response to what you're radiating, the energy you're sending out in the form of your patterns of thoughts. Put your attention on the real source of all that you experience. Money is your thoughts manifested. Look at the cause of everything you experience. Look to and at your patterns of thought.

PROSPERITY SPREE: Spend your daily cheque from the Universe on new items.

VIBRATING ⊙ ABUNDANCE	
DATE: _____	
PAY TO THE ORDER OF _____ FIVE MILLION	$5,000,000 /100 DOLLARS
Universe INC. 444 Abundance Way Billionaire View, CA 000000	*The Universe* AUTHORIZED SIGNATURE
⑆111222⑆ ⑈33⑉3444⑈ ⑆555	

Money as Acknowledgment: Remind yourself today that there is no such thing as cost, expense, bill, or payment. Whatever you purchase today, whatever your money flows toward, your out-flow is a part of the abundance cycle. Remind yourself as you go about your day, that all there is, is a gesture of acknowledgment for the services and items you are receiving. Money is a way of saying "thank you for these services and goods" for everything you are receiving.

Your I-Have-it List: take a moment today to make a list of everything you have in your life that benefits you – from the clothes you wear, the dollars and cents in your wallet or account, to the dishes in your cupboard, take a moment to take stalk of the abundance already in your experience. Give your attention to what it is you already have.

POSITIVE PROJECTION: If you notice your mind projecting a future time of lack, create and use "what if" statements to anticipate abundance.

APPRECIATE! APPRECIATE! APPRECIATE!

::: YOU HAVE MORE THAN ENOUGH OF EVERYTHING FOR TODAY! :::

DAY 28

THOUGHT of the day: It's not your job, employer, business, bank, partner, parent or other providing you with money. These appearances are all outcomes, acceptable channels you've allowed for receiving the money you've materialized. The source of all the money in your life is your own consciousness. What is it that you've been thinking and believing about money that it has come in the way that it has for you? As you've thought, so you've experienced. As you put your attention on your thought patterns and change what needs changing, you will naturally increase the flow of abundance in your life.

PROSPERITY SPREE: Spend your daily cheque from the Universe on new items.

```
         VIBRATING ⊙ ABUNDANCE
                        DATE: _____
PAY TO THE
ORDER OF                          $6,000,000
              SIX MILLION         /100 DOLLARS

Universe INC.
444 Abundance Way                 The Universe
Billionaire View, CA 000000       AUTHORIZED SIGNATURE
         | |"111222| |'"33'"3444| |"555
```

Money as Acknowledgment: Remind yourself today that there is no such thing as cost, expense, bill, or payment. Whatever you purchase today, whatever your money flows toward, your out-flow is a part of the abundance cycle. Remind yourself as you go about your day, that all there is, is a gesture of acknowledgment for the services and items you are receiving. Money is a way of saying "thank you for these services and goods" for everything you are receiving.

Your I-Have-it List: take a moment today to make a list of everything you have in your life that benefits you – from the clothes you wear, the dollars and cents in your wallet or account, to the dishes in your cupboard, take a moment to take stalk of the abundance already in your experience. Give your attention to what it is you already have.

POSITIVE PROJECTION: If you notice your mind projecting a future time of lack, create and use "what if" statements to anticipate abundance.

APPRECIATE! APPRECIATE! APPRECIATE!

::: YOU HAVE MORE THAN ENOUGH OF EVERYTHING FOR TODAY! :::

DAY 29

THOUGHT of the day: Everything that you see right now as your dollars and source of dollars is just an effect or materialization of your past convictions. As you expand your ideas of what money is and what's available to you, you are encoding every layer of your being with thoughts that are vibrating abundance and wealth. The Universe will match that change in your vibration or consciousness.

PROSPERITY SPREE: Spend your daily cheque from the Universe on new items.

```
          VIBRATING ⊙ ABUNDANCE
                       DATE: _____
PAY TO THE
ORDER OF                             $7,000,000
              SEVEN MILLION          /100 DOLLARS

Universe INC.
444 Abundance Way
Billionaire View, CA 000000          The Universe
                                 AUTHORIZED SIGNATURE
         | |˚111222| |˚˚33˚˚˚3444| |˚555
```

Money as Acknowledgment: Remind yourself today that there is no such thing as cost, expense, bill, or payment. Whatever you purchase today, whatever your money flows toward, your out-flow is a part of the abundance cycle. Remind yourself as you go about your day, that all there is, is a gesture of acknowledgment for the services and items you

are receiving. Money is a way of saying "thank you for these services and goods" for everything you are receiving.

Your I-Have-it List: take a moment today to make a list of everything you have in your life that benefits you – from the clothes you wear, the dollars and cents in your wallet or account, to the dishes in your cupboard, take a moment to take stalk of the abundance already in your experience. Give your attention to what it is you already have.

POSITIVE PROJECTION: If you notice your mind projecting a future time of lack, create and use "what if" statements to anticipate abundance.

APPRECIATE! APPRECIATE! APPRECIATE!

::: YOU HAVE MORE THAN ENOUGH OF EVERYTHING FOR TODAY! :::

DAY 30

THOUGHT of the day: When you vibrate abundance, when you radiate thoughts of being abundant consistently outward, the Universe will rearrange itself to mirror your new vibrational output. There is no other cause in your life, everything that becomes visible to you is a materialization of your dominant vibrational output.

PROSPERITY SPREE: Spend your daily cheque from the Universe on new items.

```
          VIBRATING · ABUNDANCE
                      DATE: _____
PAY TO THE
ORDER OF                       $8,000,000
              EIGHT MILLION    /100 DOLLARS

Universe INC.
444 Abundance Way                The Universe
Billionaire View, CA 000000      AUTHORIZED SIGNATURE
               ||"111222||"'33'"3444||"555
```

Money as Acknowledgment: Remind yourself today that there is no such thing as cost, expense, bill, or payment. Whatever you purchase today, whatever your money flows toward, your out-flow is a part of the abundance cycle. Remind yourself as you go about your day, that all there is, is a gesture of acknowledgment for the services and items you

are receiving. Money is a way of saying "thank you for these services and goods" for everything you are receiving.

Your I-Have-it List: take a moment today to make a list of everything you have in your life that benefits you – from the clothes you wear, the dollars and cents in your wallet or account, to the dishes in your cupboard, take a moment to take stalk of the abundance already in your experience. Give your attention to what it is you already have.

POSITIVE PROJECTION: If you notice your mind projecting a future time of lack, create and use "what if" statements to anticipate abundance.

APPRECIATE! APPRECIATE! APPRECIATE!

::: YOU HAVE MORE THAN ENOUGH OF EVERYTHING FOR TODAY! :::

DAY 31

THOUGHT of the day: Give more and more thought to the abundance of energy around you and within you. Think of all the vibrating particles in the whole Universe. Reach outward with your mind and see the innumerable packets of energy that make up this Universe. Think of this infinite pool of energy that is in your constant view. Look around you even in your immediate surroundings. Look at all the energy that has materialized as the objects around you, the space you're in, the furniture you're using. It's vast. It's endless. And there is always much more of it than you can see flowing and materializing in this very instant. Abundance is really all there is.

PROSPERITY SPREE: Spend your daily cheque from the Universe on new items.

```
╔══════════════════════════════════════════╗
║        VIBRATING ⊙ ABUNDANCE             ║
║                         DATE: _____  ║
║ PAY TO THE                                ║
║ ORDER OF                      $9,000,000 ║
║           NINE MILLION        /100 DOLLARS║
║                                           ║
║ Universe INC.                             ║
║ 444 Abundance Way              The Universe║
║ Billionaire View, CA 000000  AUTHORIZED SIGNATURE║
║      | |"111222| |"'33"'3444| |"555      ║
╚══════════════════════════════════════════╝
```

Money as Acknowledgment: Remind yourself today that there is no such thing as cost, expense, bill, or payment. Whatever you purchase today, whatever your money flows toward, your out-flow is a part of the abundance cycle. Remind yourself as you go about your day, that all there is, is a gesture of acknowledgment for the services and items you are receiving. Money is a way of saying "thank you for these services and goods" for everything you are receiving.

Your I-Have-it List: take a moment today to make a list of everything you have in your life that benefits you – from the clothes you wear, the dollars and cents in your wallet or account, to the dishes in your cupboard, take a moment to take stalk of the abundance already in your experience. Give your attention to what it is you already have. What are all the ways that you are abundant today?

POSITIVE PROJECTION: If you notice your mind projecting a future time of lack, create and use "what if" statements to anticipate abundance.

APPRECIATE! APPRECIATE! APPRECIATE!

::: YOU HAVE MORE THAN ENOUGH OF EVERYTHING FOR TODAY! :::

DAY 32

    THOUGHT of the day: What's materializing in your world and as your world cannot change without a shift in your consciousness, in the vibration you predominately radiate. Lasting change comes when you've irreversibly altered the source of your manifested environment – your own practiced patterns of thought of what's available to you in every instant.

    PROSPERITY SPREE: Spend your daily cheque from the Universe on new items.

VIBRATING ⊙ ABUNDANCE	
DATE: _____	
PAY TO THE ORDER OF TEN MILLION	$10,000,000 /100 DOLLARS
Universe INC. 444 Abundance Way Billionaire View, CA 000000	*The Universe* AUTHORIZED SIGNATURE
||"111222||"33"'3444||"555	

    Money as Acknowledgment: Remind yourself today that there is no such thing as cost, expense, bill, or payment. Whatever you purchase today, whatever your money flows toward, your out-flow is a part of the abundance cycle. Remind yourself as you go about your day, that all there is, is a gesture of acknowledgment for the services and items you

are receiving. Money is a way of saying "thank you for these services and goods" for everything you are receiving.

Your I-Have-it List: take a moment today to make a list of everything you have in your life that benefits you – from the clothes you wear, the dollars and cents in your wallet or account, to the dishes in your cupboard, take a moment to take stalk of the abundance already in your experience. Give your attention to what it is you already have.

POSITIVE PROJECTION: If you notice your mind projecting a future time of lack, create and use "what if" statements to anticipate abundance.

APPRECIATE! APPRECIATE! APPRECIATE!

::: YOU HAVE MORE THAN ENOUGH OF EVERYTHING FOR TODAY! :::

DAY 33

THOUGHT of the day: It is your knowledge of what abundance is and how abundant you are that translates itself into the experiences of dollars in your life. You are constantly creating and living out your core truths and convictions – your practiced patterns of thought. Who are you? How abundant are you? What kind of abundance can come into your life? When?

PROSPERITY SPREE: Spend your daily cheque from the Universe on new items.

VIBRATING ⊙ ABUNDANCE	
DATE: _____	
PAY TO THE ORDER OF FIFTEEN MILLION	$15,000,000 /100 DOLLARS
Universe INC. 444 Abundance Way Billionaire View, CA 000000	*The Universe* AUTHORIZED SIGNATURE
ⅼⅼ"711222ⅼⅼ"'33'"3444ⅼⅼ"555	

Money as Acknowledgment: Remind yourself today that there is no such thing as cost, expense, bill, or payment. Whatever you purchase today, whatever your money flows toward, your out-flow is a part of the abundance cycle. Remind yourself as you go about your day, that all there is, is a gesture of acknowledgment for the services and items you are receiving. Money is a way of saying "thank you for these services and goods" for everything you are receiving.

Your I-Have-it List: take a moment today to make a list of everything you have in your life that benefits you – from the clothes you wear, the dollars and cents in your wallet or account, to the dishes in your cupboard, take a moment to take stalk of the abundance already in your experience. Give your attention to what it is you already have.

POSITIVE PROJECTION: If you notice your mind projecting a future time of lack, create and use "what if" statements to anticipate abundance.

APPRECIATE! APPRECIATE! APPRECIATE!

::: YOU HAVE MORE THAN ENOUGH OF EVERYTHING FOR TODAY! :::

DAY 34

THOUGHT of the day: You are already an expression of Infinite Wealth. You are an individuation of the Abundant Source of this Universe. You've always been abundant. You've always had the infinite resources of the Universe available to you. You ARE abundance. You ARE prosperity. You ARE the wealth of the Universe. Train your mind to see through this lens and your natural inheritance will become visible to you in every way and at all times – endlessly.

PROSPERITY SPREE: Spend your daily cheque from the Universe on new items.

```
              VIBRATING ⊙ ABUNDANCE
                            DATE: _____
PAY TO THE
ORDER OF                                   $20,000,000
              TWENTY MILLION               /100 DOLLARS

Universe INC.
444 Abundance Way                          The Universe
Billionaire View, CA 000000                AUTHORIZED SIGNATURE
              | |"111222| |"33"'3444| |"555
```

Money as Acknowledgment: Remind yourself today that there is no such thing as cost, expense, bill, or payment. Whatever you purchase today, whatever your money flows toward, your out-flow is a part of the abundance cycle. Remind yourself as you go about your day, that all there is, is a gesture of acknowledgment for the services and items you are receiving. Money is a way of saying "thank you for these services and goods" for everything you are receiving.

Your I-Have-it List: take a moment today to make a list of everything you have in your life that benefits you – from the clothes you wear, the dollars and cents in your wallet or account, to the dishes in your cupboard, take a moment to take stalk of the abundance already in your experience. Give your attention to what it is you already have.

POSITIVE PROJECTION: If you notice your mind projecting a future time of lack, create and use "what if" statements to anticipate abundance.

APPRECIATE! APPRECIATE! APPRECIATE!

::: YOU HAVE MORE THAN ENOUGH OF EVERYTHING FOR TODAY! :::

DAY 35

THOUGHT of the day: The energy that builds all things is present every which way you turn. This energy is the all-providing source of everything you experience. Everything that has manifested in your experience is made of or materialized out of this unclassifiable source. And everything that has come has done so in response to your expectation and allowing. As you expand on your ideas of what you expect to receive, what you are capable of letting into your life, this energy will materialize as that in your experience in expected and unexpected ways.

PROSPERITY SPREE: Spend your daily cheque from the Universe on new items.

```
         VIBRATING ⊙ ABUNDANCE
                        DATE: _____
PAY TO THE
ORDER OF                         $30,000,000
           THIRTY MILLION        /100 DOLLARS

Universe INC.
444 Abundance Way                The Universe
Billionaire View, CA 000000      AUTHORIZED SIGNATURE
              |  |"111222|  |"'33"'3444|  |"555
```

Money as Acknowledgment: Remind yourself today that there is no such thing as cost, expense, bill, or payment. Whatever you purchase today, whatever your money flows toward, your out-flow is a part of the abundance cycle. Remind yourself as you go about your day, that all there is, is a gesture of acknowledgment for the services and items you are receiving. Money is a way of saying "thank you for these services and goods" for everything you are receiving.

Your I-Have-it List: take a moment today to make a list of everything you have in your life that benefits you – from the clothes you wear, the dollars and cents in your wallet or account, to the dishes in your cupboard, take a moment to take stalk of the abundance already in your experience. Give your attention to what it is you already have.

POSITIVE PROJECTION: If you notice your mind projecting a future time of lack, create and use "what if" statements to anticipate abundance.

APPRECIATE! APPRECIATE! APPRECIATE!

::: YOU HAVE MORE THAN ENOUGH OF EVERYTHING FOR TODAY! :::

DAY 36

THOUGHT of the day: The Universe is forever expressing its true nature of unfaltering abundance. You're not making it do this. It's just what it does. Your only work is to recognize the truth of this so that this endless abundance can materialize into your experience. Be convinced that abundance is all there is. Look through and past what's materialized out of your scarcity thinking. See the evidence of abundance all around you and train yourself into seeing that ever-present abundance predominately. Your abundance will grow in proportion to your expanded vision. As you change your thoughts, as you change your lens, you change your vibrational output – you change what you radiate. And this abundant Universe will reciprocate that raised vibration back into your experience through easy channels.

PROSPERITY SPREE: Spend your daily cheque from the Universe on new items.

VIBRATING ⊙ ABUNDANCE	
DATE:	
PAY TO THE ORDER OF FORTY MILLION	$40,000,000 /100 DOLLARS
Universe INC. 444 Abundance Way Billionaire View, CA 000000	*The Universe* AUTHORIZED SIGNATURE
‖¹111222‖ ‖⁻³³⁻⁻³444‖ ‖⁻555	

Money as Acknowledgment: Remind

yourself today that there is no such thing as cost, expense, bill, or payment. Whatever you purchase today, whatever your money flows toward, your out-flow is a part of the abundance cycle. Remind yourself as you go about your day, that all there is, is a gesture of acknowledgment for the services and items you are receiving. Money is a way of saying "thank you for these services and goods" for everything you are receiving.

Your I-Have-it List: take a moment today to make a list of everything you have in your life that benefits you – from the clothes you wear, the dollars and cents in your wallet or account, to the dishes in your cupboard, take a moment to take stalk of the abundance already in your experience. Give your attention to what it is you already have.

POSITIVE PROJECTION: If you notice your mind projecting a future time of lack, create and use "what if" statements to anticipate abundance.

APPRECIATE! APPRECIATE! APPRECIATE!

::: YOU HAVE MORE THAN ENOUGH OF EVERYTHING FOR TODAY! :::

DAY 37

THOUGHT of the day: The only cause of your prosperity is you. You, your Consciousness, is the source of all your wealth. The supply of the Universe is endless and undiscriminating. Your experience of that endless supply depends on how much of it you allow through the thoughts you've practiced – through the beliefs you've encoded your being with.

The more you practice thoughts of abundance, the more abundance you let in. The more you think in terms of having more than enough, always being provided for, the more you experience just that. Think of your thoughts as magnetic. The more your consciousness is filled with thoughts of scarcity, the more you magnetize scarcity into your life. The more your consciousness is filled with thoughts of abundance, the more abundance you magnetize into your experience.

You and what types of thoughts your consciousness is filled with is the common thread and cause in everything you experience.

PROSPERITY SPREE: Spend your daily cheque from the Universe on new items.

```
          VIBRATING ⊙ ABUNDANCE
                          DATE: _____
PAY TO THE
ORDER OF                              $50,000,000
              FIFTY MILLION          /100 DOLLARS

Universe INC.
444 Abundance Way                    The Universe
Billionaire View, CA 000000         AUTHORIZED SIGNATURE
           ||"111222||"33"'3444||"555
```

Money as Acknowledgment: Remind yourself today that there is no such thing as cost, expense, bill, or payment. Whatever you purchase today, whatever your money flows toward, your out-flow is a part of the abundance cycle. Remind yourself as you go about your day, that all there is, is a gesture of acknowledgment for the services and items you are receiving. Money is a way of saying "thank you for these services and goods" for everything you are receiving.

Your I-Have-it List: take a moment today to make a list of everything you have in your life that benefits you – from the clothes you wear, the dollars and cents in your wallet or account, to the dishes in your cupboard, take a moment to take stalk of the abundance already in your experience. Give your attention to what it is you already have.

POSITIVE PROJECTION: If you notice your mind projecting a future time of lack, create and use "what if" statements to anticipate abundance.

APPRECIATE! APPRECIATE! APPRECIATE!

::: YOU HAVE MORE THAN ENOUGH OF EVERYTHING FOR TODAY! :::

DAY 38

THOUGHT of the day: Money is the essence of your dominant patterns of thought-output returned to you. Your thought-output isn't only in what you're thinking but in everything you're expressing. There is a pattern of thought behind everything you say and do, so you're constantly and continuously radiating out a particular quality of energy – a particular frequency. Put another way, money is the frequency of your dominant vibrational output returned to you. Money is visible evidence of the frequency or signal you predominately broadcast outward. Change that signal, and you absolutely change what visible form is returned to you. You've always been in this seat of power – the power is in the thoughts you choose.

PROSPERITY SPREE: Spend your daily cheque from the Universe on new items.

```
        VIBRATING ⊙ ABUNDANCE
                    DATE: _____
PAY TO THE                     $60,000,000
ORDER OF
           SIXTY MILLION       /100 DOLLARS

Universe INC.
444 Abundance Way                 The Universe
Billionaire View, CA 000000   AUTHORIZED SIGNATURE
        ||"111222| |"33"3444| |"555
```

Money as Acknowledgment: Remind

yourself today that there is no such thing as cost, expense, bill, or payment. Whatever you purchase today, whatever your money flows toward, your out-flow is a part of the abundance cycle. Remind yourself as you go about your day, that all there is, is a gesture of acknowledgment for the services and items you are receiving. Money is a way of saying "thank you for these services and goods" for everything you are receiving.

Your I-Have-it List: take a moment today to make a list of everything you have in your life that benefits you – from the clothes you wear, the dollars and cents in your wallet or account, to the dishes in your cupboard, take a moment to take stalk of the abundance already in your experience. Give your attention to what it is you already have.

POSITIVE PROJECTION: If you notice your mind projecting a future time of lack, create and use "what if" statements to anticipate abundance.

APPRECIATE! APPRECIATE! APPRECIATE!

::: YOU HAVE MORE THAN ENOUGH OF EVERYTHING FOR TODAY! :::

DAY 39

THOUGHT of the day: What does the vibration of abundance feel like? There's no secret to this. How do you feel when you have enough money to do something you want? You feel free. You feel appreciative. You feel excited. You feel eager. You feel unlimited. You feel good.

Such an uplifted or positive feeling is the feeling you want to achieve in yourself. A consciousness of abundance is a consciousness filled with thoughts that feel good. Bring yourself to dwell on the things, thoughts, or experiences that generate these good feelings within you. Let these good feelings be your predominant broadcast as you go about your day. When you change your energetic or vibrational signal, you change the signal of the experiences that come to you. Put another way, you must be the vibrational signal you want to experience.

PROSPERITY SPREE: Spend your daily cheque from the Universe on new items.

```
          VIBRATING ⊙ ABUNDANCE
                         DATE: _____
PAY TO THE
ORDER OF                              $70,000,000
              SEVENTY MILLION         /100 DOLLARS

Universe INC.
444 Abundance Way                      The Universe
Billionaire View, CA 000000         AUTHORIZED SIGNATURE
              |  |"111222|  |'"33'"3444|  |"555
```

Money as Acknowledgment: Remind yourself today that there is no such thing as cost, expense, bill, or payment. Whatever you purchase today, whatever your money flows toward, your out-flow is a part of the abundance cycle. Remind yourself as you go about your day, that all there is, is a gesture of acknowledgment for the services and items you are receiving. Money is a way of saying "thank you for these services and goods" for everything you are receiving.

Your I-Have-it List: take a moment today to make a list of everything you have in your life that benefits you – from the clothes you wear, the dollars and cents in your wallet or account, to the dishes in your cupboard, take a moment to take stalk of the abundance already in your experience. Give your attention to what it is you already have.

POSITIVE PROJECTION: If you notice your mind projecting a future time of lack, create and use "what if" statements to anticipate abundance.

APPRECIATE! APPRECIATE! APPRECIATE!

::: YOU HAVE MORE THAN ENOUGH OF EVERYTHING FOR TODAY! :::

DAY 40

THOUGHT of the day: If your focus is on "getting money", you're flowing your attention on a condition, on an outcome. Money is an outcome. Flow your attention on being abundance, on being wealth itself. Be abundance. Practice and anchor thoughts of abundance in your consciousness. Encode your being with thoughts of abundance. The outcome will show up in ways that astound you.

PROSPERITY SPREE: Spend your daily cheque from the Universe on new items.

```
            VIBRATING ⊙ ABUNDANCE
                          DATE: _____
PAY TO THE
ORDER OF                                $75,000,000
            SEVENTY FIVE MILLION        /100 DOLLARS

Universe INC.
444 Abundance Way                       The Universe
Billionaire View, CA 000000             AUTHORIZED SIGNATURE
            ||"111222| |'"33'"3444| |'555
```

Money as Acknowledgment: Remind yourself today that there is no such thing as cost, expense, bill, or payment. Whatever you purchase today, whatever your money flows toward, your out-flow is a part of the abundance cycle. Remind yourself as you go about your day, that all there is, is a gesture of acknowledgment for the services and items you are receiving. Money is a way of saying "thank you for these services and goods" for everything you are receiving.

Your I-Have-it List: take a moment today to make a list of everything you have in your life that benefits you – from the clothes you wear, the dollars and cents in your wallet or account, to the dishes in your cupboard, take a moment to take stalk of the abundance already in your experience. Give your attention to what it is you already have.

POSITIVE PROJECTION: If you notice your mind projecting a future time of lack, create and use "what if" statements to anticipate abundance.

APPRECIATE! APPRECIATE! APPRECIATE!

::: YOU HAVE MORE THAN ENOUGH OF EVERYTHING FOR TODAY! :::

PART III: YOUR NEW PATTERN

Your practiced pattern of thought, the story that plays out in your mind, on every subject is everything that you experience. Your story is your constant vibrational radiation, what you continuously radiate outward. Your practiced story is your point of asking, the vibration the Universe or Unified Field endlessly mirrors and reflects back to you. Until there is a change in that story, until there is a shift in the pattern you keep active about what abundance is and how it can come to you, whatever change you force on the surface will disintegrate before your eyes. Your mind, your consciousness, your dominant vibration, will always come through and materialize.

Any change that occurs on the surface level, any success you gain and allow without changing the root cause of your experience does not last. You can paint an old house as many times as you want, but it will still remain and fall like an old house in its structure. There's nothing rooted to hold that superficial change in place. The change must come from within as a shift in your very outlook and understanding of what the source of your abundance is.

It isn't about how hard you work. It isn't about the state of the economy. It isn't about where you came from. It isn't about sweat. It isn't about labor. It isn't about anything you've taught yourself it's about. It isn't about anything that you do on the physical action level.

    The stream of consciousness contained in this book is allowing you to shape a new story, a new vibrational template, within yourself. This new energetic pattern is everything. This new story is your building block, your foundation, your blueprint. This new story and understanding, this new shift is what determines what and how you now predominately think about yourself and your world, what you predominately say about yourself and your world, and what you do inside yourself and in your world.

    This story is what determines what you constantly radiate or emanate outward on every level of your being. This new story is what the Universe will begin responding to, what the Universe has already begun responding to when you decided to embark on your transformative journey. This new story is what determines how you experience your abundance and what the infinite energy of the Universe now materializes itself into as your dollars, as your wealth. All things grow out of your practiced habits of thought, the very energies you're constantly encoding your entire being with.

    Every single behavior that you take part in, every word you speak, is an effect of the thoughts you have been practicing. The root of all that you experience and express is the silent story you have within yourself, the story on loop in your mind. When the story in your mind shifts to be about your unlimited nature in every aspect of your being, everything about you from your mind outward will shift to materialize or mirror this internal expansion, this internal shift in your consciousness that you have deliberately brought forth.

You are no longer working with the effects or the outcomes of your thoughts. You are no longer working with the conditions and circumstances materializing out of your thoughts. You are working with the root cause itself. You are working with the foundation. You are working with the template, the blueprint. You are creating permanent change in your consciousness.

Can you think yourself into wealth?

Can you think yourself into the kind of abundance you've dreamed of?

Your criteria for abundance, how to have it, if you can have it, how much of it you can have, how you relate to it and how it relates to you, are only thoughts you have practiced. You're the only one that can decide what you can and cannot do, what you can and cannot have and who you ultimately can and cannot be. The Universe does not limit you. You're the only one that can determine how much wealth you are capable of materializing, and what you yourself are capable of, through the belief-sets or rule-sets you've set up for yourself. You create what you believe. You live out the expectations you have formed. You decide.

DECLARATION OF INNER POWER

Use the following declaration as a template to create your own. Take a moment each day to remind yourself that all the power of change and expansion is within yourself, it's always been within yourself.

I now recognize that the only power in my experience is my own consciousness. Where I once held external conditions and circumstances to be the cause and power in my world, now I know with every fiber of my being that my own consciousness is what matters.

My consciousness is what materializes as every moment I experience and this is true for my experience of abundance, wealth and prosperity. I need only decide to take my power back, I need only stop assuming that things in the outer world have power over my experiences. And so I do that now.

My consciousness is what determines what comes to me. My consciousness is what determines how I experience currency, dollars, money. My own consciousness is the source of my finances and so it is here that I do my work.

I am now shifting into a consciousness of wealth.

I am now shifting into a consciousness of abundance.

I am now shifting into a consciousness of prosperity.

And each and every day I grow and grow in my capacity to allow more. I allow more for the good of my well-being. I allow more for the benefit of those around me. I allow more for the prosperity of my world. As I am rich in consciousness, so will I be in my world. As I am prosperous in consciousness, so shall I be in my world. And so I am. Here and Now.

And so it is.

NEW MONEY THOUGHTS

Pay attention to what, if anything, comes up for you as you interact with these positive thoughts and beliefs about money and about your relationship with money. As you read and review these lists, where you encounter any level of internal disturbance, where you find yourself contradicting, rejecting or negating the statements, is where you can identify the resistance that is there. To resist a positive perspective on money on any level is to interfere with the flow of it in your life. Let yourself clear out and unravel any pocket of resistance you discover and uncover.

Ask yourself: why am I reacting this way? What have I been believing instead? What emotions accompany what I've been believing?

You can also rewrite and reframe the statements to better suit your desired perspective. You can use the list of positive thoughts provided as a jumping off point to access and write out your own versions. The statements in the list are examples, a small snapshot of the millions of positive thoughts around money floating about that are all available to you.

Explore, uncover, and release all of your resistance to an increased flow of abundance in the form of money, and tune into the patterns of thinking that will make you want to smile, skip and dance whenever you think about money.

ABUNDANT THOUGHTS

Train yourself to continue to think along the lines of abundance. Let the frequency or energy pattern you create within your consciousness be in line with the abundance you desire to experience.

- There is always more than enough money.
- I have more than enough of everything for today, for this week, for this month, for this year, for the rest of my life.
- There is always more of everything I want coming.
- My outrageous abundance is guaranteed.
- I always have more money coming to me.
- My source of money is unlimited.
- I have so many predictable and unpredictable channels of money.

- I am the center of abundance.
- I've always been deserving of financial abundance.
- I've deserved unlimited abundance my whole life.
- My prosperity is inevitable.
- My financial freedom is guaranteed.
- There is an endless stream of abundance constantly flowing to me.
- My prosperity is right now unlimited.
- I've always been a magnet for endless abundance.
- I expect to live and experience my outrageous abundance in every moment.
- Unending Abundance is my true nature.
- Abundance is all there is.
- Wealth is all there is.
- My source and supply of abundance is vast and unlimited.
- My unfailing abundance is coming to me through innumerable channels.
- My source and supply of prosperity, of money, is inexhaustible.
- The source of my abundance is immediate.

- My chain of abundance is endless.
- Right here and right now I have access to dollars beyond my imagination.
- I am blessed beyond measure.
- My abundance comes to me in increasing quantities.
- I am blessed beyond my fondest dreams.
- There is an eruption of abundance in my life right now.
- The Universe is always determined to shower me with more than I've asked for.
- I am blessed beyond anything I've ever dreamed of.
- My financial sources are infinite.
- I have an unlimited bank account, an unlimited vast reservoir of abundance, right here and right now.
- There is an Infinite Intelligence tending to the details of my prosperity, I don't need to give thought to tomorrow.
- It is raining abundance in my world.
- I am completely unrestricted in my outrageous abundance.
- I trust in my ability to allow unrestricted abundance.

- I release all resistance to my well-being.
- I fly free and soar into my limitless abundance.
- I radiate abundance in every moment.
- My every cell pulses and vibrates to the resonance of limitless wealth.
- I have absolute and total financial freedom right here and right now.
- I am a vortex of inexhaustible abundance.
- I exist in Infinite Abundance.
- The stream of abundance is endless and unfaltering.
- I've always been wealthy beyond limit.
- I've always had access to the infinite resources of the Universe.
- Every day in every way I grow richer and richer.
- All the abundance of the Universe is available for my use.

MORE POSITIVE MONEY BELIEFS

1) There is an endless supply of money.
2) Money is divine, sacred, and pure.
3) Money is light and consciousness.
4) Money is love and energy.

5) I am one with the energy of prosperity.

6) Being rich and wealthy is divine and pure.

7) Money is in abundant supply in this Universe.

8) Money comes into my life quickly, easily, and frequently.

9) It's easy to save money.

10) Spending money is so much fun.

11) Receiving money is so much fun.

12) I don't have to hang onto money because there's always more coming.

13) There are lots of loving and amazing people with lots of money.

14) There are rich human beings who are honest and authentic all over the world.

15) The economy is getting even better and better in every moment.

16) Money can come into my life abundantly, effortlessly and easily.

17) I can work less and earn so much more. Yes, I can!

18) Rich people all over the world are generous and wonderful.

19) As money is Spirit in form, money is 100% spiritual.

20) It is divine to have a lot of money all the time.

21) There are lots of spiritual people who are rich and well.

22) It's easy to be rich.

23) There are millions of happy healthy rich people in the world.

24) Credit is divine and pure.

25) I can easily go from making little money to making lots of money.

26) It's easy to have multiple sources of income other than a job.

27) It's easy to make lots of money from investments.

28) There is no limit to how much I can earn in a week, month, or year.

29) Amazing opportunities come quickly and frequently all the time.

30) Success is always knocking on my door and following me around everywhere I go.

YOU AND MONEY

31) I deserve success after success in this life.

32) I have amazing unique talents and abilities.

33) I am a unique and necessary part of the whole.

34) I matter.

35) Others love and appreciate me.

36) I am first on my list of people to love and appreciate.

37) I am a wonderful human being.

38) I deserve happiness, love, success, and all the good things in this life.

39) I am worthy as a human being.

40) I am enough just as I am.

41) I'll definitely succeed. My success is inevitable.

42) I deserve an abundance of money in my life.

43) I am absolutely worthy of making good money.

44) It's really okay to make more than other's in my life.

45) The more I make, the more I gain.

46) I can afford anything I want any time.

47) I'm wonderful at managing my money. I am a money expert.

48) I am such a success.

49) I have lots of people in my life who are supportive of my success.

50) The more I make, the more supportive loving people I bring into my life.

51) There are so many people who are cheering for me to succeed.

52) It's easy to find a good job. It's easy to find work.

53) I am completely debt free.

54) My bank account will always be overflowing with money.

55) Money doesn't make me forget who I really am.

56) Money doesn't change my values.

57) Money lets me celebrate my abundant and wonderful nature.

58) Money supports me in living out my values.

59) I celebrate other's having lots of money. Their wealth makes me happy.

60) I will always be able to make lots of money.

61) I am wonderful at making money.

62) I am wonderful at managing my money.

63) There are always ways to get ahead.

64) My ability to make money is all about my consciousness.

65) I love sharing my wealth because I always have more coming.

66) No matter my profession, career, or work I really don't have to struggle hard to earn a living.

67) I can charge as much as I want for my services.

68) People will happily pay whatever I charge. I'm worth it.

69) Making money is just so easy.

70) Money is the easiest thing to demonstrate in this world.

71) I am so happy with what I have in the bank.

72) My credit card bill never has a balance on it.

73) I love paying my bills. I so appreciate the services I receive and so I pay with joy.

74) I love saying "thank you" for the services I receive with money. I love writing checks for services I have received.

75) I deserve a big pay raise.

76) I love elevating my financial worth.

77) I love spending money on myself and others.

78) I can have a six figure income, it's easy.

79) I can be a millionaire.

80) Financial freedom has always been mine to experience.

81) I am worth a big monthly salary and yearly figure.

82) I greatly value my own potential.

83) I love thinking about money.

84) Money is so much fun!

85) The money I have has nothing to do with anything other than my consciousness.

EXPANDING YOUR ABUNDANCE METER

86) I am worth so much even without money.

87) I love acknowledging my worth.

88) I love dreaming big, it feels so good to consider the amazing possibilities for me in my world.

89) I adore myself for who I am every day.

90) I can easily be rich and happy and successful.

91) I have always been able to manifest abundance. I am a master manifest-er of abundance.

92) My life is one of joy and celebration.

93) My life is so full.

94) I can do what I love and make really good money easily.

95) My passions and my creativity can abundantly support me.

96) Life was always meant to be a breeze.

97) I live in a loving Universe that loves, values and appreciates me.

98) I live in a loving Universe that loves and supports me in every moment.

99) I am of great value to my world.

100) I am a great contribution to my world.

101) I am a wonderful presence in this world.

102) The world desires whatever I have to offer.

103) Everything I touch turns to gold.

104) I am always so lucky.

105) Miracles are the norm for me.

106) I will always have more than enough.

107) I will always be provided for each and every moment.

108) I feel safe in my wealth.

109) I feel secure in my abundance and in my abundant nature.

110) It is so wonderful to be rich, wealthy, and prosperous.

111) The future has so many amazing and wonderful experiences in store for me.

112) Abundance, wealth, and prosperity meet me in every corner.

113) I love that I am abundantly celebrating each and every day of my life.

114) Abundance was always my birthright.

115) The more money I have, the more I find myself doing more for my world.

116)   I was always meant to have it all: a loving family, work I love to do, amazing friends, wonderful health, and lots of money.

117)   I love having more than I need!

118)   I love my never-ending stream of wealth and prosperity.

119)   I am so blessed with abundance and great fortune.

120)   I love being wealthy, prosperous, and abundant.

121)   I always have been and always will be a powerful magnet for unlimited wealth.

ANTICIPATING ABUNDANCE

Continuously allow yourself to project a reality of abundance. You can train yourself into expecting an endless flow of dollars by a slight shift in the practiced patterns of thought you have created. Use "what if" statements and other projective statements to allow yourself to anticipate and expect abundance.

- What if there's more money coming?
- What if more money becomes visible to me today?
- What if money comes into my hands in this very next instant?
- What if my practiced thoughts are the source of all my wealth?
- What if it really has nothing to do with outside conditions?
- What if I right now tune into more money than I've ever dreamed of?
- What if I look at and appreciate the money I do have right now?
- What if I stop anticipating lack?
- What if I deliberately anticipate abundance?
- What if the financial change I desire shows up in the next instant?
- What if an amazing opportunity is right around the corner?

- ◉ What if everything changes for the better in an instant?
- ◉ What if I receive more money than I've ever dreamed of right now?
- ◉ What if unexpected sources of income surround me in the next breath?
- ◉ What if the Universe has already answered all my prayers?
- ◉ What if the Universe has already planned out my increased levels of prosperity and well-being?
- ◉ What if I just keep getting more and more and more?

Every aspect of your physical experience is a creation of your consciousness. Your abundance and experience of prosperity is no exception. Tune into the abundant nature of who you really are deliberately. Thought by thought allow yourself to shift into the abundant you that already lives in this moment, Here & Now.

You can.

You are the sole author, definer, and perceiver of all that you make manifest in and as your personal physical reality.

AUTHOR'S NOTE

Dear Reader,

 I want to thank you for reading. I hope the ideas and guidance in this workbook helped you to access or reaffirm the wisdom and understanding already within you. My intention with all my work is that it helps, supports and reinforces your knowing of your power and reminds you of just how cosmically blessed, connected and loved you are. The basis of all that we are is a love that is powerful and a power that is loving.
 If you enjoyed this book and have a minute to spare, I would really appreciate a short review on Amazon. It is reviews from readers like you that help new readers connect to my work to find the help, support and reinforcement they need in their own empowerment and transformation journey.

Thank you again for joining me in catching up to our collective expansion.

Infinite Blessings to you in all that you are and all that you do.

With great love and gratitude,
Kidest OM
http://infinite-life.com

P.S. If you'd like to receive ongoing reminders on your power and potential, you can connect to my YouTube and Facebook channels. I update them fairly regularly with reminders, new insights and more tools, tips and guidance.

http://facebook.com/KidestOm

http://youtube.com/KidestOm

ABOUT THE AUTHOR

Kidest OM is the author of several books and publications on the power and primacy of consciousness. Kidest received her B.A. in Psychology and for almost a decade worked in the research field seeking to understand the power of perception, cognition, psyche development and experiences in shaping individuals.

In search of more empowering, holistic and integrative approaches, she has extensively studied, practiced, and mastered various technologies and exploratory maps of consciousness which she now uses to facilitate the desired shifts in her client's as well as her own day to day experiences.

She has hosted and created numerous informative radio shows and videos on the subject of consciousness and reality creation reaching thousands of viewers and listeners worldwide.

Currently living in the Pacific North West, Kidest describes life on Vancouver Island as the perfect backdrop to conversations on consciousness.

Find more from Kidest OM in all Amazon stores.

Made in the USA
Middletown, DE
01 November 2019